ACOL BRIDGE MADE EASY

More and more people are finding out what a great joy it is to be able to play bridge. You can learn at any age, but one thing is sure. You will wish you had started earlier.

Bridge is the most stimulating, most intriguing, most fascinating, most challenging of all card games. It will give you more lasting pleasure than any other recreation because of its unending variety. You will never tire of bridge.

And yet, bridge is easy . . . easy enough to learn to play a respectable game. *Acol Bridge Made Easy* will have you playing bridge in just a few short hours. Time will pass most quickly and agreeably for you. Once you start playing, you will want to play again and again. Study *Acol Bridge Made Easy* closely and you will have a sound grounding in the game. Happy bridging.

by RON KLINGER *in the Master Bridge Series*

* GUIDE TO BETTER CARD PLAY
GUIDE TO BETTER ACOL BRIDGE
100 WINNING BRIDGE TIPS
50 WINNING DUPLICATE TIPS
PLAYING TO WIN AT BRIDGE
THE MODERN LOSING TRICK COUNT
FIVE-CARD MAJORS
BRIDGE WITHOUT ERROR
IMPROVE YOUR BRIDGE MEMORY
WORLD CHAMPIONSHIP PAIRS BRIDGE
BASIC BRIDGE: A Guide to Good Acol Bidding and Play
ACOL BRIDGE MADE EASY
TEACH YOUR CHILD BRIDGE
ACOL BRIDGE FLIPPER
BASIC ACOL BRIDGE FLIPPER
DUPLICATE BRIDGE FLIPPER
FIVE-CARD MAJORS BIDDING FLIPPER
MODERN LOSING TRICK COUNT FLIPPER
STANDARD BRIDGE FLIPPER
MASTER OPENING LEADS
MASTER PLAY AT TRICK 1
MASTER CUE BIDDING TO SLAMS
MASTER DOUBLES

with Hugh Kelsey
INSTANT GUIDE TO STANDARD BRIDGE

with David Bird
KOSHER BRIDGE

* Winner of the 1991 *Book of the Year Award*
of the American Bridge Teachers' Association

ACOL BRIDGE MADE EASY

Ron Klinger

LONDON
VICTOR GOLLANCZ LTD
in association with
PETER CRAWLEY
1992

First published in Great Britain October 1986
in association with Peter Crawley
by Victor Gollancz Ltd
14 Henrietta Street, London WC2E 8QJ
Second impression May 1987
Third impression May 1988
Fourth impression December 1989
Fifth impression September 1990
Sixth impression February 1992

British Library Cataloguing in Publication Data
Klinger, Ron
  Acol bridge made easy.–(The Master
  bridge series)
  1. Contract bridge–Bidding
  I. Title   II. Kelsey, H.W.   III. Series
  795.41'52   GV1282.4

  ISBN 0-575-03931-0

Photoset and printed in Great Britain by
WBC Print Ltd., Bridgend

To Keri

Contents

Bridge is easily the world's most popular card game. It is played in about a hundred countries and has an estimated following of over 50 million players.

Bridge is becoming more and more popular as increasing leisure enables more and more people to take up worthwhile and challenging recreations. Bridge is unrivalled when it comes to card games that offer a significant challenge.

Bridge is a social asset and is played by both sexes. It has numerous advantages over other recreations and sports. It can be played under any weather conditions and can be played under the most severe physical handicaps. The deaf can play bridge and even the blind can play. A blind bridge player competed in the 1978 World Championships!

Bridge is not an 'old person's game' and children of seven years and younger have been taught to play. More and more young people are taking up bridge and players in their twenties have won world championships.

On the other hand, age is no barrier to bridge which can be both enjoyed and played successfully at any age. Players in their seventies have won world titles competing against all ages and likewise, players in their eighties have won national championships against all comers. The main complaint of those who do not take up the game early in life is the regret that they did not take it up sooner.

Chapter 1

FROM WHIST TO BRIDGE

A SERIES OF FUN GAMES FOR BEGINNERS

What type of game is bridge?

There are two basic families of card games. In one, the aim is to form combinations of cards, e.g. Gin Rummy, Canasta, where the aim is to collect groups such as three nines, four fives, or runs in the same suit, such as 7-8-9 of clubs, Q-J-10-9 of hearts, etc. Contract Bridge belongs to the other in which the aim is to win *tricks*. Other games in the bridge family are Whist, Solo, Five Hundred and Euchre.

The form of bridge played today is called Contract Bridge, which can be played socially (rubber bridge) or competitively (duplicate bridge). It was devised in 1925, prior to which the form of bridge played was Auction Bridge which became popular at the beginning of the 20th century. Bridge itself developed at the end of the 19th century from the game of Whist which can be traced back to the 17th century. The word 'bridge' has its ancestry in the Russian word 'Biritch' or Russian Whist.

Bridge is played by four people, two playing as partners, against the other two. Partners sit opposite each other. You will need a card table, four chairs, two packs of cards (though you can manage with one pack), score pads and pencils.

How many cards are in the pack?

A pack (or deck) of 52 cards is used. There are no jokers. There are four suits: spades ♠, hearts ♡, diamonds ♢ and clubs ♣. Each suit has thirteen cards, the highest being the ace, followed by the king, queen, jack, 10, 9, 8, 7, 6, 5, 4, 3, down to the 2 which is the lowest.

How do we choose partners?

You may agree to play in certain partnerships, for example husband and wife against the other couple (probably the worst possible arrangement), but unless there is some other agreement, it is usual to draw for partners. This is done by spreading out the pack, face down, and each player picking a card. The two who draw the higher cards play as partners against the other two, normally for one or two 'rubbers'.

After a rubber has been completed, cards are drawn again to form two new partnerships. If, in drawing for partners, two or more cards of the same rank are turned up, then the tie is split according to suit, the suits ranking from the highest, spades, through hearts and diamonds to the lowest, clubs.

For example, A, B, C and D are drawing for partners. The cards turned up are A: ♢8   B: ♠J   C: ♠5   D: ♡8. What are the partnerships? (*Answer:* B-D against A-C)

A wit has said that in bridge there is good news and bad news. The good news is that you always have a partner. The bad news is . . . exactly the same.

Who deals?

The person who draws the highest card has the right to choose seats (the most comfortable one) and which pack of cards to use for dealing (for the superstitiously inclined, who might think one of the packs is luckier), and also becomes the dealer on the first hand. The next dealer will be the person on the left of the previous dealer and so on in clockwise rotation.

The cards are shuffled by the person on the dealer's left. The shuffler puts the cards face down on the right. ("If you would avoid a fight, place the cards upon your right.") The dealer picks up the shuffled pack and passes it across the table to the player on dealer's right to 'cut' (take a number of cards from the top of the pack and place these cards face down next to the remainder). The dealer completes the 'cut' (place the remainder of the pack on top of the ones cut to make a complete pack again) and then 'deals' the cards, one at a time, face down, in clockwise direction, starting with the player on the left, until all 52 are dealt.

How many cards will each player have? Who receives the last card? (*Answers:* 13; the dealer)

It is customary etiquette not to pick up your cards until the dealer has finished dealing . . . this allows the dealer equal time to study the cards and also allows a misdeal to be corrected. During the deal, the dealer's partner is shuffling the other pack in readiness for the next deal . . . that is why two packs are used, in order to speed up the game. After the shuffling is finished, the cards are put on the shuffler's right, ready for the next dealer.

```
              N
      W      □      E
              S
```

Suppose that in this diagram South is the dealer.

(a) Who shuffles the pack with which South is going to deal?
(b) Who cuts this pack?
(c) Who receives the first card dealt?
(d) Who is shuffling the other pack while South is dealing?
(e) Where is the other pack placed after it is shuffled?
(f) Who will be the next dealer?

Answers: (a) West   (b) East   (c) West   (d) North
(e) On North's right   (f) West

The start of play

After picking up your 13 cards, sort them into suits . . . it is usual to separate the red suits from the black suits and also to put your cards in order of rank in each suit. Each bridge hand consists of two distinct parts: the bidding (also called the 'auction') and the play. The bidding starts with the dealer but more about the bidding later. It is worthwhile playing a number of games first which do not involve any bidding. These games do illustrate the principles of play and once the ideas involved in the play are understood and absorbed, the objects and rules of the bidding are much easier to understand.

GAME 1 – NO-TRUMPS WHIST

Each player receives 13 cards. Opposite players are partners. There is no bidding, no dummy and no trump suit. The player on the left of the dealer makes the 'opening lead', that is, places one card face up on the table. Each player in turn in clockwise order plays a card face up. That group of four cards, one from each player, is called a *trick*.

In no-trumps, a trick is won by the highest card of the suit led.

The partnership that wins a trick gathers up the four cards and places them in a neat pile face down. The player who won the trick starts the play to the next trick, i.e. 'leads to the next trick'. Play continues until all 13 tricks have been played and each side then counts up the number of tricks won. The side winning more than 6 tricks is the winner and is the only side that scores points.

The first card played to a trick is called the 'lead'. Each subsequent player must play a card of the same suit as the lead, if possible. This is known as 'following suit'. The basic law of play is: *You must follow suit if possible*. If you are unable to follow suit at no-trumps, you should discard those cards which you judge to be worthless. When it is your turn to play, you may play a high card or a low card, as you choose, but *if possible, you must follow suit*. Even though you could play a high card to win the trick, this might be a foolish move if you can tell partner's card is going to win the trick anyway.

Scoring:

We play a **rubber** of bridge. A rubber is **best of three games**. The first side to score **100 points or more** in tricks won scores a **game**. The first side to win two games wins the rubber. A 2-0 win scores 700 bonus points, a 2-1 wins scores 500.

The trick score in NO-TRUMPS is:
30 points for each trick won over six, plus 10.

So 7 tricks (making 1NT) is worth 40 points, 8 tricks (2NT) is worth 70, 9 tricks (3NT) is worth 100, and so on.

A bridge scoresheet looks like this:

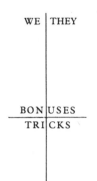

```
WE  |  THEY



BONUSES
─────────
TRICKS
```

Trick scores are written below the line, bonus scores are written above the line. At the end of a game, a line is ruled across both columns and both sides start the next game from zero again. At the end of a rubber the scores in each column are tallied and the higher scoring side is the winner.

The difference between the two scores is rounded off to the nearest 100 (e.g. 870 goes to 900, 820 goes to 800; 850 would go down to 800) and the score is then entered as the number of 100s won or lost.

For example, if you won by 900, your scoresheet will read "+9" while their scoresheet would record "–9".

Strategy at no-trumps:

Prefer to lead your longest suit and keep on with that suit. When the others run out, your remaining cards in that suit will be winners, since they cannot win the trick if they cannot follow suit. As players lead their own long suit, it is best to return partner's led suit, unless you have a strong suit of your own, and usually avoid returning a suit led by the opposition.

The card to lead: Top card from a sequence of three or more cards headed by the ten or higher (e.g. from K-Q-J-5, lead the K; from J-10-9-8, lead the J). The top five cards in each suit – A, K, Q, J, 10 – are called the 'honour cards'. Lead top of a sequence only when the sequence contains one or more honours.

Lead fourth-highest (fourth from the top) where the long suit has no such three-card or longer sequence (e.g. from K-J-8-4-3, lead the 4).

GAME 2 – TRUMPS WHIST

Each player receives 13 cards. The top card of the other pack is turned up as the trump suit. This card is left face-up during the play to remind each of the players which suit is trumps. There is still no bidding and no dummy.

In trumps, a trick without a trump card is won by the highest card of the suit led, but a trick with a trump card is won by the highest trump.

Throughout the play, you are still obliged to follow suit, of course. If you are unable to follow suit at trumps, you are permitted to 'ruff' (i.e. play a trump card – to ruff simply means to trump). However, you are not obliged to do so and you may choose to discard a worthless card instead of ruffing. Since you are not forced to ruff when you are out of a suit, you will decide whether to ruff or whether to discard. It is sensible to ruff a winning card played by an opponent but it might be unwise to ruff if partner's card is going to win the trick anyway. Remember, you are partners.

Scoring:

The trick score in TRUMPS for each trick over six is:
30 points if spades or hearts are trumps.
20 points if diamonds or clubs are trumps.

So if hearts are trumps, making 1 ♡ (7 tricks) is worth 30, 2 ♡ (8 tricks) is worth 60, 3 ♡ (9 tricks) is worth 90, and so on. If clubs are trumps, 7 tricks (1 ♣) would score 20, 8 tricks (2 ♣) would score 40, 9 tricks (3 ♣) would score 60 and so on.

Strategy at trumps:

Prefer to lead a short suit such as a singleton (one card in a suit) or a doubleton (two cards in a suit – lead top card from a doubleton) or a strong suit (headed by a sequence or by A-K). With none of these, a trump lead is reasonable if you have a lot of trumps (five or more) or you might start with the best of your other suits.

GAME 3 – TRUMPS AND NO-TRUMPS

Each player receives 13 cards. Opposite players are partners. The top card of the other pack is turned face up. If a 2, 3 or 4 is turned up, the game is to be played in no-trumps. If a higher card is turned up, the suit of the face-up card is to be the trump suit for that deal. This card is left face-up during the play to remind the players of the trump suit or no-trumps.

The play and scoring is the same as Game 1 and 2. Game 3 is a combined version of Games 1 and 2.

Additional Strategy:

Second player to a trick commonly plays low, third player to a trick usually plays high, trying to win the trick if possible. If partner's card has already won the trick, you need not beat partner's card in fourth seat.

GAME 4 – DEALER'S WHIST

Each player receives 13 cards. The dealer, after examining the 13 cards held and without consulting partner, declares the trump suit or no-trumps. This gives the dealer some control over the selection of trumps, whereas in Games 2 and 3, the card turned up as trumps (or no-trumps) is purely a matter of luck. When you are a dealer, it is best to choose as your trump suit only a suit with five or more cards. With no five-card or longer suit, usually prefer to choose no-trumps.

Play:

Same as before. There is no dummy.

Scoring:

Same as before.

GAME 5 – PARTNERSHIP WHIST

This is the same as Game 4 except that the dealer and the dealer's partner discuss whether to play in trumps or no-trumps. This gives the dealer's side a much better chance of discovering a good trump suit than when the dealer alone makes the choice.

The dealer and dealer's partner make one suggestion ('bid') at a time, nominating a trump suit or no-trumps. The dealer makes the first bid. If partner agrees, that decides the trump suit or no-trumps. If partner disagrees, partner makes an alternative suggestion. If no trump suit is agreed after three turns each, the hand is to be played with no-trumps.

[17]

Play:
Same as before. There is still no dummy.

Scoring:
Same as before.

GAME 6 – DECLARER'S WHIST

Each player counts the high card points held, using **A = 4, K = 3, Q = 2, J = 1**. Starting with the dealer, each player calls out the total number of points held. The player who has most points becomes the 'declarer'. If there is a tie for the most points held, the declarer will be the dealer (if involved in the tie) or the player nearest the dealer (if the dealer is not involved in the tie . . . nearest goes according to clockwise direction).

The rest of the game is the same as Game 4 except that the declarer (rather than the dealer) declares what is to be trumps or whether play is to be at no-trumps.

GAME 7 – DUMMY WHIST WITHOUT POINTS

Each player receives 13 cards. *The partner of the dealer puts all 13 cards face up in suits on the table as the dummy hand.* The declarer is the partner of the dummy and declares the trump suit or no-trumps.

To choose a trump suit, the suit should have 8 or more cards in the combined hands. If more than one trump suit is available, choose a major suit (spades or hearts) rather than a minor suit (diamonds or clubs), as the majors score more. If the suits are both majors or both minors, choose the longer, or if both have the same length, choose the stronger. If there is no suit which has 8 or more trumps together, usually prefer to play no-trumps. Being able to see partner's hand gives the dealer's side an even better chance of finding no-trumps or the best suit for trumps.

After the trump suit or no-trumps has been declared, the player on the left of the declarer makes the first lead. The play proceeds as before but **the declarer must play both hands**. The dummy player takes no part in the play. If dummy wins a trick, the next lead comes from dummy, while if declarer wins a trick, declarer must lead to the next trick.

Scoring:

Same as usual if declarer wins seven or more tricks. However, if declarer fails to win seven tricks or more, the other side will score bonus points at the rate of 50 for each trick by which declarer failed. For example, if declarer made only four tricks, the other side would score 150 bonus points, since declarer failed by three tricks.

Bonus points are scored above the line and do not count towards scoring a game. Only the declarer side can score points towards game. Bonus points are still valuable since they count in your total points at the end of the rubber.

GAME 8 – DUMMY WHIST

Each player counts the high card points held, using **A = 4, K = 3, Q = 2, J = 1**. Starting with the dealer, each player calls out the total number of points held. The side which has more points becomes the declarer side and the partner that has more points becomes the declarer. Dummy is revealed and declarer nominates the trump suit or no-trumps. (The pack has 40 HCP. If each side has 20, redeal the hand. For a tie in the declarer side, the one nearer the dealer will be the declarer.)

The play proceeds as before: left of declarer makes the opening lead and declarer plays both dummy and his own hand.

Scoring:

If declarer scores seven tricks or more, scoring is as usual. If declarer fails to win seven tricks, the opponents score bonus points. *Only the declarer side can score points for game.* Where the declarer side has not won a game ('not vulnerable'), the opponents score 50 bonus points for each trick by which they have defeated declarer, regardless of which suit is trumps or whether no-trumps is played. Where the declarer side has won a game ('vulnerable'), the opponents will score 100 points for each trick by which they have defeated declarer.

The existence of the dummy marks off Bridge from other trick-taking games. From the first lead, each player sees half the pack (13 cards in hand + 13 cards in dummy), thus making Bridge essentially a game of skill, in contrast to the large luck factor in other games. Since the declarer side in this game will have more points than the defenders, the declarer side is more likely to succeed in taking seven or more tricks.

GAME 9 – BIDDING WHIST

Starting with the dealer, each player states the number of points held. The side with more points is the declarer side and the two partners discuss which suit shall be trumps or whether to play no-trumps. Each partner in turn suggests a trumps suit or no-trumps, until agreement is reached. This is known as the 'bidding' or the 'auction'. A bid is simply a suggestion to partner which suit you prefer as trumps or whether you prefer no-trumps.

A suggested trump suit must contain at least four cards. With no particularly long suit and no void ('void' = no cards in a suit) and no singleton (one card in a suit), it is usually best to suggest no-trumps at once. If there is no early agreement and neither partner insists on a suit, one of the partners should suggest no-trumps. After agreement, the first player to suggest the agreed trump suit (or no-trumps if agreed) is the declarer.

In the play, the player on the left of the declarer makes the opening lead *before seeing dummy*. After the lead, dummy's 13 cards are placed face up (in suits), facing declarer. Trumps go on dummy's right. The scoring is the same as for Game 8.

GAME 10 – CONTRACT WHIST + BIDDING

The early play proceeds exactly as Game 9. However, instead of needing to win just seven or more tricks, the declarer is required to win a specific number of tricks depending on the total points held by declarer and dummy:

20-22 points: 7 or more tricks in no-trumps
                8 or more tricks with a trump suit

23-25 points:	8 or more tricks in no-trumps
	9 or more tricks with a trump suit
26-32 points:	9 or more tricks with no-trumps
	10 or more tricks with ♡ or ♠ as trumps
	11 or more tricks with ♣ or ◇ as trumps
33-36 points:	12 or more tricks
37-40 points:	All 13 tricks

Play:

The opening lead is made before dummy appears.

Scoring:

The same as for Game 9, but to score points declarer must win the number of tricks stipulated or more. If not, the defenders score bonus points of 50 (declarer not vulnerable) or 100 (declarer vulnerable) for each trick by which declarer fails.

If declarer is required to win 12 tricks ('small slam') and does so, the declarer side scores an extra bonus of 500 when not vulnerable or 750 vulnerable. If declarer is required to win all 13 tricks ('grand slam') and does so, the declarer side scores an extra 1000 not vulnerable or 1500 vulnerable.

Chapter 2

OPENING THE BIDDING

How does the bidding operate?

The play is preceded by the bidding, also called 'the auction'. Just as in an auction an item goes to the highest bidder, so in the bridge auction each side tries to outbid the other for the right to play the hand. As only the declarer side can score points towards a game, each side endeavours to win the bidding in order to become the declarer side.

The dealer makes the first bid, then the player on dealer's left and so on in clockwise rotation. Each player may pass (say "No Bid") or make a bid. A player who has passed previously may still make a bid later in the auction. A bid consists of a number (1, 2, 3, 4, 5, 6 or 7) followed by a suit or no-trumps, e.g. 3 Hearts, 2 Spades, 4 No-Trumps, 7 Diamonds and so on. 'No-Trumps' means that there is to be no trump suit on the deal. Whenever a bid is made, the bidder is stating the number of tricks *above six* intended to be won in the play. The minimum number of tricks that you may contract for is seven. A bid of 1 Club contracts to make seven tricks with clubs as trumps. The number in the bid is the number of tricks to be won *over and above six tricks*. (Six tricks is not even halfway and you have to bid for more than half the tricks.) The final bid is called the 'contract'.

How many tricks must declarer win to succeed in each of the following contracts? Which suit is to be trumps?

(a) 3 Clubs (b) 4 Spades (c) 6 No-Trumps (d) 2 Hearts

(*Answers:* (a) 9, clubs (b) 10, spades (c) 12, none (d) 8, hearts)

If all players pass without a bid on the first round, there is no play, the hand is thrown in and the next dealer deals a new hand. When a player makes a bid on the first round, the auction has started and will be won by the side that bids higher. The auction is over once a bid is followed by three passes. If you make a bid and the other three players pass, you are not allowed to bid again. Your last bid has become the contract. The side that bids higher sets the trump suit (or no-trumps) and the number of tricks it has to win in the play; this is set by the final bid and the member of the side who first bid the trump suit (or no-trumps) becomes the declarer.

After a bid, any player in turn may make a *higher* bid. A bid is higher than a previous bid if it is a higher number than the previous bid (three-anything is higher than two-anything) or if it is the same number but in a higher ranking denomination. The order of ranking is:

No-Trumps
♠ Spades
♡ Hearts
◇ Diamonds
♣ Clubs

A bid of 1 Heart is higher than a bid of 1 Club. Likewise, a bid of 1 Spade is higher than a bid of 1 Heart. If you wanted to bid spades and the previous bid was 2 No-Trumps, you would have to bid at least 3 Spades. 2 Spades would not be higher than 2 No-Trumps.

(a) What is the highest bid possible?
(b) How many tricks does it undertake to make?
(c) What is the lowest bid possible?
(d) If the previous bid was 1 Spade, and you want to bid diamonds, what is the lowest bid in diamonds you can make?
(e) The previous bid was 1 Spade. Would a bid of 1 Heart be legal? What about a bid of 1 No-Trump?

(*Answers:*   (a) 7 No-Trumps   (b) Thirteen   (c) 1 Club
(d) 2 Diamonds   (e) No; Yes)

Counting points

To succeed as the declarer side, you have to win the number of tricks for which you have bid, or more. The more tricks in your contract, the harder your task. The strength of your hand is measured by the Point Count Method and whenever you make a bid, part of the message to your partner is the number of points you hold. The higher the contract, the more points you and partner need for success. The challenge in the bidding is to assess your own points accurately and to gauge partner's points from the bids partner makes so that you can assess how high you should bid.

The basic count is high card points (HCP) A = 4, K = 3, Q = 2, J = 1

Each suit contains A-K-Q-J, so each suit has 10 HCP. Thus, there are 40 HCP in the pack. These 40 HCP are shared out among the four players and so an average hand has 10 HCP.

Bidding for game:

When holding 26 points or more between you and partner, the partnership should bid a game. (The game bids are those that score 100 points or more: 3NT, 4♡, 4♠, 5♣ and 5♢.)

Therefore, do not pass in the bidding until some game is reached if the partnership *could* have 26 points or more.

With 26 points together, game is a good chance.

With 25 points together, game is a fair chance.

With 24 points or less, game prospects are poor.

Opening the bidding:

An opening bid is the first bid in the auction. Pass is not a bid.

The standard approach for opening is:

0-11 points:	Do not open the bidding. Pass initially.
12-19 points:	Open with 1-of-a-suit, unless the hand fits 1NT.
20-up:	Open with 2-of-a-suit, unless suitable for 2NT or 3NT.

Opening bids of 2-of-a-suit, 2NT and 3NT are covered in Chapter 5.

GAME 11 - BIDDING MADE EASY

Each player receives 13 cards. Starting with the dealer, each player will either pass (say "No Bid") or make a bid.

These are the rules for opening the bidding:

1. With 0-11 points, pass initially. You may bid later.
2. With 12-19 points, bid a suit at the 1-level. (If the opponents have already bid, you may bid a strong suit at the cheapest level.)
3. With 20 points or more, bid a suit at the 2-level.
4. You are not permitted to bid no-trumps at your first turn, but you may bid no-trumps at your second or later turn. Any suit that you bid must contain at least four cards.

If your partner has already opened the bidding, you are the responder and the guide for responding is:

1. With 0-5 points, pass an opening bid at the 1-level, but answer an opening bid of two, even with a worthless hand.
2. With 6 or more points, answer partner's opening bid either by supporting partner's suit or by bidding your own suit. Any suit you bid must contain at least four cards and support for partner's suit also requires four cards. You are not permitted to bid no-trumps at your first turn, but you may bid no-trumps at your second or later turn.
3. With 16 or more points, reply with a jump in a new suit or if you have no suit of your own, jump-support partner's suit to game.

When you have more than one suit to bid, choose your first bid as follows, whether you are opener or responder:

1. Bid your longest suit first (not necessarily the strongest).
2. With two five-card suits, bid the higher-ranking suit first (spades is the highest-ranking suit, then hearts, diamonds, clubs).
3. If you have only one four-card suit, bid that suit. With two or three four-card suits, bid the cheapest possible suit.

The bidding continues until there are three passes after a bid. If you can work out that your partnership has at least 26 points, bid to a game of 3NT, 4♡, 4♠, 5♣ or 5♢. Prefer to choose a trump contract if you have eight or more trumps together. The declarer side is the partnership that makes the final bid (the contract) and the declarer is the member of that partnership who bid the trump suit or no-trumps first.

The play proceeds as usual: left of declarer makes the opening lead and declarer plays both dummy and his own hand.

Scoring:

As normal if declarer makes the number of tricks required in the contract. If declarer fails to win the number of tricks required, the opponents score bonus points (50 points for each trick by which declarer fell short if the declarer side is not vulnerable, 100 points per trick short of the contract if the declarer side is vulnerable).

GAME 12 – BIDDING WITH NO-TRUMPS

This game is identical to the previous game except that you may open with a bid of 1NT with 12-14 points and no short suit and you may answer 1NT to partner's opening bid with 6-9 points and no good suit to bid.

Hand patterns and hand shapes

A bridge hand contains 13 cards and the pattern of a hand is determined by the number of cards in each suit. Hand patterns are described from the longest suit to the shortest suit. For example, a 6-4-2-1 pattern means the hand contains a six-card suit, a four-card suit, a doubleton and a singleton. A 5-5-3-0 pattern means the hand contains two five-card suits, a three-card suit and a void. Give the patterns of these hands:

HAND 1	HAND 2	HAND 3
♠ A 8 5 3	♠ J 2	♠ K 6 4
♡ - - -	♡ A J 8 7 4 3	♡ 9 5 2
◇ K Q 7 6 3	◇ 8 5 4	◇ A J 9
♣ A K 9 8	♣ 3 2	♣ J 6 5 4

(*Answers:* 1: 5-4-4-0; 2: 6-3-2-2; 3: 4-3-3-3.)

There are three hand shapes, balanced, semi-balanced and unbalanced.

Balanced shapes: 4-3-3-3, 4-4-3-2 or 5-3-3-2 pattern.

These are hands which contain no void, no singleton and at most one doubleton.

Semi-balanced shapes: 5-4-2-2, 6-3-2-2 or 7-2-2-2 pattern.

These are hands which contain no void, no singleton and two or three doubletons.

Unbalanced shapes: These are all patterns other than those listed above. Unbalanced hands always contain at least one singleton or one void.

Balanced hands are usually best for no-trumps, while unbalanced hands are usually best for a trump contract, provided that a good trump suit is available. Semi-balanced hands are reasonable for no-trumps but may also end up in a trump contract if a good trump suit is available.

How many suits do I have for bidding?

We talk about hands being one-suiters, two-suiters and three-suiters. A one-suiter contains only one suit of four or more cards (e.g. 4-3-3-3, 5-3-3-2, 6-3-3-1, 7-3-2-1 patterns). A two-suiter contains two suits which have four or more cards (e.g. 5-4-2-2, 5-5-2-1, 6-4-3-0 patterns). A three-suiter has three suits with at least four cards (4-4-4-1 or 5-4-4-0 patterns). A suit should contain at least four cards to be worth bidding.

What opening bid should I choose?

If you have fewer than 12 points, pass. Do not open the bidding. If you have 20 points or more, check with Chapter 5 for your opening bid. If you have 12 to 19 points, the following principles will help you to choose the correct opening bid:

The 1NT opening shows 12-14 points and balanced shape.

If the hand fits, prefer 1NT to any other opening bid.

If the hand does not fit a 1NT opening:
  Bid your longest suit first.

With two five-card suits or two six-card suits (5-5 or 6-6 patterns), bid the higher-ranking suit first.

With four-card suits only, bid the cheapest suit. This is called bidding 'up-the-line'.

Examples of opening bids

♠ 7 6 2
♡ A K 8 3 2
◇ K Q 9
♣ K 8

You hold 15 HCP and a 5-3-3-2 pattern. The hand is a balanced one-suiter. You have more than enough to open the bidding. Open 1 Heart.

♠ A Q 8 3 2
♡ K 9 8 2
◇ 8
♣ K 8 4

You hold 12 HCP and a 5-4-3-1 pattern, an unbalanced two-suiter. Open 1 Spade, the longer suit first. If the spades are not supported, bid the hearts later.

♠ A J 8 3
♡ K Q 7 2
◇ 7
♣ A K Q 2

You hold 19 HCP and a 4-4-4-1 pattern. The hand is an unbalanced three-suiter. Open 1 Club, the cheapest suit when you hold only four-card suits.

♠ A 9 8 4
♡ K 7
◇ A J 8 4
♣ Q 6 4

You hold 14 HCP and a 4-4-3-2 pattern. The hand is a balanced two-suiter. Open 1 No-trump. When the hand fits, prefer 1 No-Trump to any other opening.

♠ A 9 8 4
♡ K 7
◇ A J 8 4
♣ A 6 4

You hold 16 HCP and a 4-4-3-2 pattern, a balanced two-suiter too strong for 1NT. Open 1 Diamond, the cheaper suit with two four-card suits (bidding 'up the line').

♠ A Q 7 5 4
♡ 8
◇ K Q 9 6 5
♣ A 2

You hold 15 HCP and a 5-5-2-1 pattern. The hand is an unbalanced two-suiter. Open 1 Spade. With two five-card suits, bid the higher ranking suit first.

♠ J 8 6 4 2
♡ 7
◇ A K Q J
♣ A K 2

You hold 18 HCP and a 5-4-3-1 pattern, an unbalanced two-suiter. Open 1 Spade, the longer suit first. The diamonds will be winners even if spades become trumps.

♠ A K 8   You hold 15 HCP and a 4-3-3-3 pattern, a
♡ K Q 3   balanced one-suiter. The 4-3-3-3 pattern is
◇ Q J 8   called a 'flat' hand. Open 1 Club. The poor
♣ 5 4 3 2   quality of the suit is not important.

♠ Q 9 7 6 2   You hold 13 HCP and a 5-5-2-1 pattern, an
♡ A K Q 5 4   unbalanced two-suiter. Open 1 Spade, the
◇ Q 3   higher suit with a 5-5 pattern. The better
♣ 7   quality of the hearts changes nothing.

A little about bridge notation

Bridge bids are written with the number first, suit next. Thus, 1NT
stands for 1 No-Trump, 1 ♠ stands for 1 Spade, 4 ♡ is 4 Hearts, 2 ◇
is 2 Diamonds, 6 ♣ is 6 Clubs, and so on. Cards are written with the
suit symbol first, card next. Thus ♠ J stands for the jack of spades,
♡ 4 stands for the 4 of hearts, ◇ 9 is the 9 of diamonds, ♣ 2 is the 2 of
clubs, and so on.

Example hands

Hand 1: Dealer North: Nil vulnerable

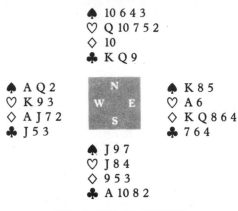

```
              ♠ 10 6 4 3
              ♡ Q 10 7 5 2
              ◇ 10
              ♣ K Q 9

  ♠ A Q 2          N          ♠ K 8 5
  ♡ K 9 3       W     E       ♡ A 6
  ◇ A J 7 2        S          ◇ K Q 8 6 4
  ♣ J 5 3                     ♣ 7 6 4

              ♠ J 9 7
              ♡ J 8 4
              ◇ 9 5 3
              ♣ A 10 8 2
```

RECOMMENDED BIDDING

West	North	East	South
	Pass	1NT	Pass
3NT	Pass	Pass	Pass

Bidding: West can count that East-West have at least 27 points.

Lead: 2 of clubs, fourth-highest from the long suit.

Play: North-South should win the first four tricks in clubs (♣ Q; ♣ K; ♣ A; ♣ 10). Declarer should win the rest, with 3 spade tricks, 2 hearts and 5 diamonds, making nine tricks. It is worth noting that 5 ◇ would fail, despite the nine-card trump fit. Balanced hands are usually best played in no-trumps.

Hand 2: Dealer East: East-West vulnerable

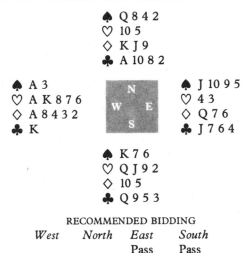

```
                    ♠ Q 8 4 2
                    ♡ 10 5
                    ◇ K J 9
                    ♣ A 10 8 2
    ♠ A 3                          ♠ J 10 9 5
    ♡ A K 8 7 6           N        ♡ 4 3
    ◇ A 8 4 3 2      W        E    ◇ Q 7 6
    ♣ K                  S        ♣ J 7 6 4
                    ♠ K 7 6
                    ♡ Q J 9 2
                    ◇ 10 5
                    ♣ Q 9 5 3
```

RECOMMENDED BIDDING

West	North	East	South
		Pass	Pass
1♡	Pass	Pass	Pass

Bidding: West opens the higher-ranking of two five-card suits. East is too weak to respond – East-West cannot have 26 points. As neither North nor South is worth a bid, West is left in 1♡.

Lead: North has no attractive lead. The 2 of spades, fourth-highest, is as good as anything.

Play: South plays the king of spades (third-hand-high) and West wins with the ace. The ace and king of hearts should be cashed followed by the ace of diamonds and another diamond. West might make seven or eight tricks.

Hand 3: Dealer South: East-West vulnerable

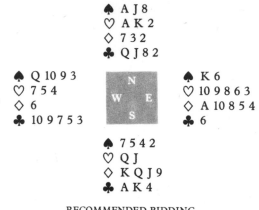

♠ A J 8
♡ A K 2
◇ 7 3 2
♣ Q J 8 2

♠ Q 10 9 3
♡ 7 5 4
◇ 6
♣ 10 9 7 5 3

♠ K 6
♡ 10 9 8 6 3
◇ A 10 8 5 4
♣ 6

♠ 7 5 4 2
♡ Q J
◇ K Q J 9
♣ A K 4

RECOMMENDED BIDDING

West	North	East	South
			1 ◇
Pass	3NT	All pass	

Bidding: South bids the cheaper of two four-card suits. North has more than enough for game and a flat hand with every suit outside diamonds well-covered, making 3NT a logical choice.

Lead: 10 of hearts, top of sequence. Do not lead a diamond, since you should prefer not to lead a suit bid by the opponents.

Play: North can count 8 instant winners (1 spade trick, 3 hearts, 4 clubs). The diamonds can provide at least two more tricks, but first the ◇ A must be dislodged. Win the ♡ Q and lead the ◇ K. Set up your extra tricks *before* cashing your sure winners.

Hand 4: Dealer West: Both vulnerable

```
                        ♠ K 8 2
                        ♡ K Q 3
                        ◇ 9 6 4 3
                        ♣ 7 6 4
  ♠ Q J 10 7 4                            ♠ 9 5
  ♡ J 8 6          N                      ♡ 10 9 7 2
  ◇ J 2         W     E                   ◇ A K Q
  ♣ A 9 8          S                      ♣ 10 5 3 2
                        ♠ A 6 3
                        ♡ A 5 4
                        ◇ 10 8 7 5
                        ♣ K Q J
```

RECOMMENDED BIDDING

West	North	East	South
Pass	Pass	Pass	1NT
Pass	Pass	Pass	

Bidding: South has a sound 1NT opening with 14 points and a flat hand. North knows North-South cannot have 26 points.

Lead: Queen of spades, top of sequence from long suit.

Play: South can count five sure tricks (2 spades and 3 hearts). Two extra tricks can be set up in clubs but to do so the ace of clubs must be knocked out. Declarer should win the spade lead and immediately lead clubs. Set up your extra tricks before cashing your sure winners. If South played the top spades and hearts before starting on the clubs, 1NT could be defeated.

Chapter 3

WEAK HAND RESPONSES
AFTER A ONE-OPENING

With 40 high card points in the pack, shared among four players, an average hand contains 10 points. Below 10 points, under average, is a weak hand. Normally you would not bid with such a hand unless partner has already made a bid.

Where partner has opened the bidding, it is possible to make a game when responder has fewer than 10 points. It will depend on the strength of opener's hand and the number of points held by responder. Reponder's weak hands are normally divided into two ranges, 0-5 points and 6-9 points.

With 0-5 points, prospects for game are too slim, but with 6 points or better, game is possible if a trump fit is found and opener has a maximum opening. The principles therefore are:

Responder has 0-5 points: pass.
Responder has 6-9: bid (but keep it low!).

Where responder is strong enough to reply, the response chosen will depend on the opening bid. Responding to 1NT is not the same as responding to a suit opening since opener's point count is different, with the 1NT opening being 12-14 and the other one-openings being 12-19.

After a 1NT opening, game is too unlikely if responder has 6-10 points. With a balanced hand and up to 10 points, pass the 1NT opening.

Where responder's hand is unbalanced or where responder holds a long suit, it is preferable to play in a trump part-score rather than in 1NT. Even though game has little or no chance, it is worth responding when you have a long suit, since it makes sense to be in the part-score that has the best chance of success. With such a hand, responder should bid a suit at the two-level. Bid your longest suit first, while with two five-card suits, bid the higher suit first. A two-level suit reply to a 1NT opening is a weak response promising at least five cards in the suit bid.

Where the opening bid is 1 ♣, 1 ♢, 1 ♡ or 1 ♠, a responding hand of only 6-9 points is not encouraging. Opener may have just 12 points, so that the partnership might have barely half the points in the pack or a little more. In this situation, responder should keep the bidding at a low level. You may support opener's suit by raising it to the two-level (e.g. 1 ♡: 2 ♡), but otherwise make a bid only at the one-level (e.g. 1 ♡: 1 ♠). With 6-9 points responder should certainly make a bid, since opener might have 19 points and then a game contract is a reasonable chance. However, if opener has only 12 points or so, it will be tough to make more than seven or eight tricks, and that is why it pays to bid conservatively with just 6-9 points. The guideline is:

With 6-9 points, raise opener's suit to the two-level or respond at the one-level in a suit or 1NT. Do not bid a new suit at the two-level with less than 10 points.

When responder bids a suit over opener's suit, responder is promising no more than a four-card suit. Responder's suit might be longer or responder might have more than one suit to show. The guidelines for responder are the same as for opener:

Bid your longest suit first.

With 5-5 or 6-6 shape, bid the higher suit first.

With only 4-card suits, bid the cheapest possible suit.

A suit need not be strong to bid it, but it must contain at least four cards. This is to enable partner to work out when a decent trump suit exists for the partnership. An adequate trump fit means a suit where the partnership has at least eight trumps.

When a partner bids a suit once, partner is promising at least a four-card suit. To support this suit, you need four trumps to ensure that the partnership has at least eight trumps. This applies both for responder supporting opener's suit and for opener supporting responder's suit.

When you are supporting partner's suit, voids, singletons and doubletons become valuable holdings because you are able to trump once you run out of a suit. The shorter your holding in a suit outside trumps, the more valuable your hand and you should count extra points for shortages when supporting partner or when partner has supported you. The Short Suit Count is:

Void	=	**5 points**
Singleton	=	**3 points**
Doubleton	=	**1 point**

The 5-3-1 count is added only after a trump fit is known. Add the shortage points for each shortage held, for example, add 6 points for two singletons or 2 points for two doubletons.

With a choice of responses, prefer to raise opener's major, bid your own suit at the one-level or raise opener's minor. If none of these actions is available, reply 1NT as a last resort.

Examples of weak hand responses

♠ K 7 6 2
♡ 8 7
♢ 6 5 3
♣ 7 6 4 2

You hold only 3 points and should pass any opening bid from 1♣ to 1NT. Even if partner opened 1♠, your hand is worth only 4 points (one for the doubleton).

♠ A 7 2
♡ 6 5 4
♢ Q 9 5 2
♣ 7 4 3

You should pass 1NT (no chance for game), but respond to any other 1-opening. Over 1♣, bid 1♢. Over 1♢, raise to 2♢. Over 1♡ or 1♠, bid 1NT.

♠ Q 8 7 4 2
♡ K 2
♢ 6 5
♣ J 8 7 2

Over 1NT, bid 2♠, promising at least five spades. Over 1♣, 1♢ or 1♡, bid 1♠ (show the spades rather than raise clubs). Over 1♠, raise to 2♠.

♠ A 9 8 4
♡ K J 6 5
♢ 8 4
♣ 7 6 2

Over 1NT, you should pass (no real chance for game). Over 1♣ or 1♢, bid 1♡ (four-card suits are bid up-the-line). Raise 1♡ to 2♡ and raise 1♠ to 2♠.

Rebids by the opener

Opener is guided by the prospect of the partnership having enough points for game. The requirements are:

For 3NT, you and partner need 26 points.

For 4♠ or 4♡, you and partner need 26 points and at least 8 trumps between you.

For 5◇ or 5♣, you and partner need 29 points and at least 8 trumps between you.

If the partnership might have 26 points, opener keeps on bidding. If the opener can tell that 26 points together is out of the question, then opener may pass if satisfied with responder's last bid. If opener dislikes responder's last suggestion, opener may make some other bid even though it is known that the partnership cannot have 26 points.

♠ A J 8 4 3
♡ K 9 7 5 4
◇ A Q
♣ 6

You opened 1♠, partner responded 1NT (6-9 points). The partnership does not hold 26 points, but you dislike NT because of your unbalanced hand. Do not pass 1NT. Rather bid 2♡, telling partner that you would prefer to play the hand in spades (your first suit) or in hearts (your other suit). Responder is expected to pass 2♡ if responder prefers hearts, but if responder has a preference for spades, it makes sense to rebid 2♠.

If the opener can tell that the partnership has 26 points, the opener can bid game if certain of the correct game contract (remembering that a good trump suit requires at least eight trumps together) or can make a jump rebid (a jump is a bid of one more than necessary) to indicate a strong hand.

♠ A Q 6
♡ A J 8
◇ K 7 5 3
♣ K J 8

You opened 1◇, partner responded 1NT (6-9 points). A quick calculation tells you the partnership has 24-27 points. Game is possible but not certain. Bid 2NT, asking partner to bid on with a maximum 1NT reply (8-9 points) and pass with a minimum (6-7 points). If opener had only 15-16 points, it would be logical to pass 1NT.

[37]

♠ A Q 7 6
♡ A K 9 8 6
♢ A Q
♣ 8 2

You have opened 1 ♡. What is your rebid if partner responded   (a) 2♡?   (b) 1♠?

In each case, you know that partner has at least 6 points. You are worth 21 points, counting one for each doubleton. You can also tell in each case that the partnership has a good trump fit, so rebid 4 Hearts in (a) and 4 Spades in (b).

There are two important principles for opener's rebid:

Where responder has changed suit, opener must bid again. Responder's change of suit is said to be a 'forcing bid'.

With a minimum opening (less than 16 points), opener should rebid at the cheapest level if unable or unwilling to pass responder's bid. Minimum bids show minimum hands, jump bids show strong hands.

For opener's rebid, opener may choose any of these actions:

Raise responder's suit with four trumps in support.

Bid no-trumps with a balanced hand.

Bid a new suit with at least four cards in that suit.

Bid the first suit again if it is at least five cards long.

When a suit is bid initially, only four cards are promised but if it is mentioned again, it must contain at least five cards. If it were bid for a third time, it would contain at least six cards. These rules enable partner to gauge when the partnership has a suit with eight or more trumps.

There are two ways that responder can deduce that opener holds at least a *five*-card suit. One we have just seen is where opener bids the same suit again. Rebidding a suit promises at least five cards in the suit. However, there is also another way: if opener's second bid is in a new suit which is lower-ranking than opener's first suit, then opener must have at least five cards in the first suit. This is because of the rule that with four-card suits we bid them up-the-line, cheaper suit first.

Suppose opener has bid 1 ♠ and after your reply of 1NT, opener rebids 2♣. (Incidentally, in bridge notation, this would be written 1♠: 1NT, 2♣.) You can tell that if opener is bidding correctly, opener will have at least *five* spades and at least *four* clubs, because if opener had only *four* spades and four clubs, the correct opening would have been 1♣ and not 1♠.

If opener bids suits 'up-the-line' at the one-level, such as 1♣: 1♡, 1♠, opener may have just four-card suits but if opener bids suits 'down-the-line' (e.g. 1♡: 1♠, 2♢), opener will have at least five cards in the first suit and four or more cards in the second bid suit.

Examples of opener's rebids

♠ A J 7 2
♡ 7 6
♢ A Q J 4 3
♣ J 9

You opened 1♢ and have a minimum opening. If partner responds 1♡, rebid 1♠. Raise a 1♠ response to 2♠. Over 1NT, rebid 2♢. There is little point in bidding 2♠ since there are no reasonable prospects for game and partner does not have a spade suit. Partner would have bid 1♠ to show the major suit rather than respond 1NT. If responder raises 1♢ to 2♢, opener should pass.

♠ A K 8 6
♡ 7
♢ A Q J 6 2
♣ K 4 3

You opened 1♢ and have a good hand. Over a response of 1♡, rebid 1♠. You are not certain of the best spot yet. Over 1♠, raise to 4♠. You are sure spades is the best suit and you are worth 20 points with spades as trumps, because of your singleton. Over a response of 1NT or 2♢, rebid 2♠. There are chances for game and while partner does not have length in spades, your best move is to describe your hand (a diamond-spade two-suiter) and indicate better than a minimum opening. Partner will realise you have a strong opening – with a minimum, you would not have bid beyond 2♢.

♠ A Q 7
♡ K Q 2
◇ 8 7 3
♣ K J 7 2

You opened 1♣ and hold 15 HCP, a moderate balanced hand. If partner replies 1◇ or 1♡ or 1♠, you should rebid 1NT. If partner replies 1NT or 2♣, pass.

♠ A Q 7
♡ A J 8
◇ A J 4
♣ Q 9 7 2

You opened 1♣ and hold 18 HCP, a strong balanced hand. If partner replies 1◇ or 1♡ or 1♠, jump-rebid to 2NT. Over a reply of 1NT or 2♣, rebid 2NT.

♠ A 9 4 3
♡ A J 8 6
◇ - - -
♣ A Q 6 3 2

You opened 1♣ and hold an unbalanced three-suiter. Over a reply of 1◇, rebid 1♡ ('up-the-line'). Over 1♡ or 1♠, jump to 4♡ or 4♠ (the void makes you worth 20).

♠ 7
♡ K Q J
◇ A K 6 5 3
♣ A Q 8 6

You opened 1◇ and have a powerful, un-balanced two-suiter. Over 1♡ or 1♠ or 1NT, make a jump rebid of 3♣. Over 2◇, jump to 5◇.

♠ A
♡ 8 7 2
◇ Q J 3
♣ A Q 9 7 4 2

You opened 1♣ and have a minimum, unbalanced one-suiter. Over 1◇ or 1♡ or 1♠ or 1NT, rebid 2♣. Over 2♣, pass. Prospects for game are too remote.

♠ A
♡ 8 7 2
◇ A Q 3
♣ A Q J 7 4 2

You opened 1♣ and have a strong, un-balanced one-suiter. Over 1◇ or 1♡ or 1♠ or 1NT, make a jump-rebid of 3♣. Over a raise to 2♣, raise again to 3♣.

Examples of responder's rebids

♠ A J 8 4
♡ Q 9 4 3
◇ 7 2
♣ 8 6 4

Imagine partner opened 1♣ and you responded 1♡, up-the-line. If opener rebids 1NT or 2♣ or 2♡, you should pass. If opener rebids 1♠, you may raise to 2♠.

♠ A 7
♡ Q 7 3
◇ Q 9 6 5 2
♣ 8 7 6

Imagine partner opened 1♣ to which you responded 1◇. If opener rebids 1♡ or 1♠, you should rebid 1NT. Over a 1NT or 2♣ rebid, you should pass.

♠ K 9 8 7 6 4
♡ A Q 6 4 2
♢ 3
♣ 2

Imagine partner opened 1♣ to which you responded 1♠. Over a rebid of 1NT, bid 4♡. Partner should pass (preference for hearts) or rebid 4♠ (preference for spades).

♠ J 3
♡ K 8 7 6 5 4
♢ J 6
♣ J 3 2

Partner opened 1♣ and you responded 1♡. Over a rebid of 1♠ or 1NT, you should rebid 2♡. Over a rebid of 2♣ or 2♡, you should pass.

♠ A 8 7
♡ K 8 4 3
♢ Q 9 7
♣ 7 6 2

Partner opened 1♣ and you responded 1♡. Over 1♠, bid 1NT. Over 1NT or 2♣ or 2♡, pass. Over any strong rebid by opener, you should bid to a game.

Example hands

Hand 5: Dealer North: Nil vulnerable

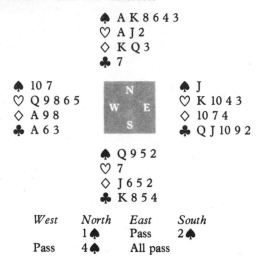

$\spadesuit$ A K 8 6 4 3
$\heartsuit$ A J 2
$\diamondsuit$ K Q 3
$\clubsuit$ 7

$\spadesuit$ 10 7
$\heartsuit$ Q 9 8 6 5
$\diamondsuit$ A 9 8
$\clubsuit$ A 6 3

$\spadesuit$ J
$\heartsuit$ K 10 4 3
$\diamondsuit$ 10 7 4
$\clubsuit$ Q J 10 9 2

$\spadesuit$ Q 9 5 2
$\heartsuit$ 7
$\diamondsuit$ J 6 5 2
$\clubsuit$ K 8 5 4

West	North	East	South
	1$\spadesuit$	Pass	2$\spadesuit$
Pass	4$\spadesuit$	All pass	

Bidding: After receiving the raise, North revalues to 20 points (add 3 for a singleton after receiving support). With South's 6-9, North has enough for game and bids it straight away.

Lead: $\clubsuit$Q, top of sequence, is best.

Play: North should ruff the second round of clubs and draw trumps in two rounds. Declarer could then lead the $\diamondsuit$ K to knock out the ace and set up extra winners there *or* cash the $\heartsuit$ A followed by ruffing the two heart losers in dummy. Declarer will make 11 tricks, losing just one trick in each minor.

Hand 6: Dealer East: North-South vulnerable

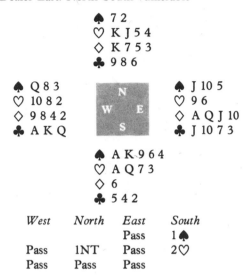

♠ 7 2
♡ K J 5 4
♢ K 7 5 3
♣ 9 8 6

♠ Q 8 3
♡ 10 8 2
♢ 9 8 4 2
♣ A K Q

♠ J 10 5
♡ 9 6
♢ A Q J 10
♣ J 10 7 3

♠ A K 9 6 4
♡ A Q 7 3
♢ 6
♣ 5 4 2

West	North	East	South
		Pass	1♠
Pass	1NT	Pass	2♡
Pass	Pass	Pass	

Bidding: North dislikes spades and responds 1NT (6-9). South, not keen on no-trumps, shows the second unit with 2♡. North prefers hearts to spades and therefore passes 2♡.

Lead: West cashes the club winners.

Play: After three rounds of clubs, West should switch to a diamond, the unbid suit. When South gains the lead, South should draw trumps in three rounds, followed by ♠A, ♠K and a spade ruffed in dummy. When spades divide 3-3, South's remaining spades are winners. Making eight or nine tricks, nine if South has an entry to the spades.

Hand 7: Dealer South: North-South vulnerable

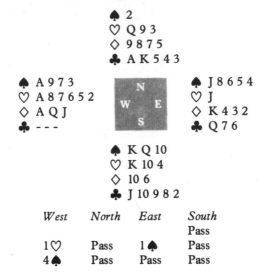

	♠ 2	
	♡ Q 9 3	
	◇ 9 8 7 5	
	♣ A K 5 4 3	

♠ A 9 7 3		♠ J 8 6 5 4
♡ A 8 7 6 5 2		♡ J
◇ A Q J		◇ K 4 3 2
♣ - - -		♣ Q 7 6

	♠ K Q 10	
	♡ K 10 4	
	◇ 10 6	
	♣ J 10 9 8 2	

West	North	East	South
			Pass
1♡	Pass	1♠	Pass
4♠	Pass	Pass	Pass

Bidding: After East responds 1♠, West revalues. With 5 for the void, West is worth 20 points and as East has shown 6 points at least, West can count enough to bid game.

Lead: Jack of clubs, top of sequence.

Play: East should ruff the club lead in dummy and cash the ace of spades. With two top trumps out, declarer is better off to abandon trumps: cash the ♡ A, ruff a heart, ruff a club, ruff a heart and ruff a club. The diamond winners are played and declarer makes 11 tricks, losing only two trump tricks. If declarer led a second trump at trick 3, declarer could be defeated.

Hand 8: Dealer West: Both vulnerable

♠ J 6 4 2
♥ A K Q
♦ 9 8 3
♣ 9 8 6

♠ A 7
♥ 7 5
♦ A Q 10 6 2
♣ K J 10 3

♠ K 9 5 3
♥ 8 4 3
♦ K 5 4
♣ Q 7 2

♠ Q 10 8
♥ J 10 9 6 2
♦ J 7
♣ A 5 4

West	North	East	South
1 ♦	Pass	1 ♠	Pass
2 ♣	Pass	2 ♦	All pass

Bidding: East bids 1 ♠ showing four spades and 6 or more points. West does not like spades and rebids 2 ♣ to show the second suit. East bids 2 ♦ to show preference for diamonds and a weakish hand. With a strong hand, East would have bid 3 ♦.

Lead: North leads the heart winners.

Play: West ruffs the third round of hearts and then draws trumps in three rounds. Clubs are led to knock out the ♣ A and declarer can make 10 tricks. If East-West were to play this deal in no-trumps (wrongly), the defence could take six tricks: three rounds of hearts won by North and later the ♣ A, followed by two more heart tricks from South.

Chapter 4

STRONG HAND RESPONSES
AFTER A ONE-OPENING

Where responder has 10 or more points, prospects for game are good. If responder knows there are enough points for game and is sure of the best contract, responder simply bids to the correct game. For example:

♠ A J 7
♡ K 7 3
◇ 8 6 4 3
♣ A K 4

Suppose partner has opened 1NT and you hold this hand. What is your response? Adding your points to partner's 12-14, you have at least 27 points together. As your hand is balanced too, bid 3NT.

Contrast this situation:

♠ A J 7 6 5 3
♡ 6
◇ A K J
♣ J 5 4

Partner has opened 1NT. Your response? Again you know that the partnership has enough points for a game (your 14 plus partner's minimum of 12) but this time your hand is not suitable for no-trumps because of the singleton. However, you can deduce that there must be at least eight spades in the partnership hands. You have six and partner would not open 1NT with a singleton or a void. Therefore, you are in a position to bid to the correct contract of 4 Spades.

However, a lot of the time responder may not be certain that there are enough points for a game or may not be able to tell whether the partnership has eight of more trumps together. In such cases, responder will not be able to bid a game yet and will have to make some other bid to investigate the possibilities.

Responder may make any bid on a strong hand other than the weak responses of 1NT or raising opener's suit to the two level. A change to a new suit forces the opener to bid again and may be made with a very strong responding hand. A jump-response or a jump-rebid by responder is a strong action which insists on game being reached (called a 'forcing-to-game' response).

Responding to 1NT

With 13 points or more, bid 3NT with a balanced hand or bid 4♡ or 4♠ with a six-card or longer suit. Include the 5-3-1 count when a known 8-card trump fit exists. A suit response at the three-level, e.g. 1NT: 3♡, shows 12 points or more (enough for game) and a *five*-card suit. Opener should support the suit with three trumps, else bid 3NT with a doubleton.

♠ A J 3
♡ K 2
◇ 9 8 7 4
♣ A J 4 2

You have opened 1NT. What action do you take if partner responds (a) 3NT? (b) 4♠? (c) 4♡? (d) 3♠? (e) 3♡?

As 3NT, 4♠ and 4♡ are games, you should pass in (a), (b) and (c). The 3♠ and 3♡ responses show five-card suits, so that opener should raise to 4♠ in (d) as there will be eight spades together, but rebid 3NT in (e) since you have only doubleton support for hearts.

Responding to a suit bid of one

10 points or more: The most common action is a change of suit initially. If you have a two-suiter or a three-suiter:

Bid your longest suit first.

With 5-5 or 6-6, bid the higher-ranking suit first.

With 4-card suits only, bid the cheapest ('up-the-line').

Specific response: A response of 2NT to 1NT or to 1♣, 1◇, 1♡ or 1♠ shows a balanced hand of 11-12 points and no four-card major. A response of 3NT to a suit opening shows 13-15 points and a 4-3-3-3 pattern with no major. Raising opener's suit from the 1-level to the 3-level (e.g. 1♣: 3♣ or 1♡: 3♡) shows 10-12 points and support for opener's suit.

If partner opened 1♣ or 1◇, prefer a major suit to a no-trump response or raising opener's minor. If partner opened 1♡ or 1♠, prefer to raise opener's major to any other response.

Rebids by opener

After a response in a new suit, opener must bid again. With support, opener should raise responder's major. If this is not possible, prefer to bid a new suit, or, if the hand is balanced, rebid in no-trumps. As a last resort, opener may rebid the first suit with five or more cards in that suit. A minimum rebid by opener shows a minimum opening, but a no-trump rebid will be 15-16 points and a jump-rebid in no-trumps shows 17 or more. Other jump-rebids by opener show a strong hand, better than a minimum 12-15 point opening.

Examples of strong responses

♠ A Q 7 3 2
♡ A K 4 3
◇ 7 2
♣ 8 6

Imagine partner opened 1♣. You know you have enough points for a game, but which game? As you cannot tell yet, bid 1♠ for the time being and await opener's rebid.

♠ A 7 6
♡ K 4 3
◇ K 8 3
♣ K J 7 6

Imagine partner opened 1◇. You have enough for a game and with balanced shape, no-trumps is attractive. Respond 3NT showing 13-15 points and a 4-3-3-3 pattern.

♠ A K Q J 8 6
♡ A K 8
◇ 7 3
♣ Q 4

Whether partner opened 1♣ or 1◇ or 1♡, you should respond 2♠, a jump in a new suit, called a 'jump-shift'. The jump-shift shows a strong suit and at least 16 hcp.

♠ 4 3
♡ 4
◇ A Q 8 7 6
♣ A K J 4 3

If partner opened 1♡ or 1♠, you should respond 2◇, the higher of two five-card suits. You have enough for a game, but which game it should be is far from clear yet.

♠ A Q 9 2
♡ 7
◇ A J 5 3
♣ K J 5 2

If partner opened 1♡, respond 1♠, (up-the-line, the cheapest of your four-card-suits). The points are there for a game but again you cannot yet tell which game is best.

Examples of opener's rebids

♠ A J 8 7 6
♡ K 9 4 3
◇ 7
♣ A Q 2

You opened 1♠ and partner responded 2NT (11-12 balanced). What is your rebid? Is the best game 4♠, 4♡ or 3NT? Bid 3♡ to tell partner you prefer spades or hearts.

♠ 7
♡ K Q 8 7 6 2
◇ A J 4
♣ Q J 3

You opened 1♡ and partner responded 2NT. Your best rebid is 4♡. You know you have enough points for game and you know there are at least eight hearts together.

♠ K Q 9 8 3
♡ Q J 6 4 2
◇ 4
♣ A J

You opened 1♠, (five-card suits are bid 'down-the-line') and partner responded 2◇. You should rebid 2♡. Your destination is still not clear, so describe your hand.

♠ J 3
♡ A K 9 6
◇ Q J 3
♣ A J 7 6

You opened 1♣ (four-card suits are bid up-the-line). If partner bids 2♠ (jump-shift), rebid 2NT. Had partner responded 1♠, you would have rebid 1NT.

♠ Q J 2
♡ K Q 9 8 7
◇ A J 4 3 2
♣ - - -

You opened 1♡ and partner responded 3♣ (jump-shift). You should rebid 3◇, just as you would have rebid 2◇ if partner's response had been 2♣.

Examples of responder's rebids

♠ A Q 7 3 2
♡ A K 4 3
◇ 7 2
♣ 8 6

Partner opened 1♣ and you responded 1♠. If partner rebids 2♣, you are still not sure of the best spot, so rebid 2♡. Had partner rebid 2♠, you would have bid 4♠.

♠ Q 7 5 3
♡ A 8 7 2
◇ Q J 4
♣ K J

Partner opened 1♣ and you responded 1♡. If partner now rebids 1NT (15-16 points), bid 3NT, while if partner bids 2♡, bid 4♡ or if partner bids 1♠, raise to 4♠.

[49]

♠ 9
♡ 6 3 2
◇ A K 8 7 2
♣ A Q 9 8

Partner opened 1♠ and you responded 2◇. If partner rebids 2♠, bid 3♣. If partner rebids 2♡, bid 3NT. Had partner opened 1♡ and rebid 2♡, you would now bid 4♡.

♠ A Q 8 7 4 2
♡ A 9 6
◇ 8
♣ 5 4 2

Partner opened 1◇ and you responded 1♠. If partner rebids 1NT or raises to 2♠, bid 4♠, but if partner rebids 2♣ or 2◇, jump to 3♠, a strong invitation to game.

♠ A 10 9 2
♡ 7
◇ A J 5 3
♣ K Q 5 2

Partner opened 1♡ and you responded 1♠. If opener now bids 2♠, bid 4♠, while if opener rebid 1NT or 2♡, bid 3NT. Had opener rebid 2♣ or 2◇, raise to 4♣/4◇.

Example hands

Hand 9: Dealer North: Nil vulnerable

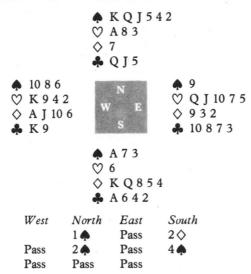

	♠ K Q J 5 4 2	
	♡ A 8 3	
	◇ 7	
	♣ Q J 5	

♠ 10 8 6		♠ 9
♡ K 9 4 2		♡ Q J 10 7 5
◇ A J 10 6		◇ 9 3 2
♣ K 9		♣ 10 8 7 3

	♠ A 7 3	
	♡ 6	
	◇ K Q 8 5 4	
	♣ A 6 4 2	

West	*North*	*East*	*South*
	1 ♠	Pass	2 ◇
Pass	2 ♠	Pass	4 ♠
Pass	Pass	Pass	

Bidding: North's 2 ♠ shows at least five spades and no support for South's diamonds. South now knows there are enough points and enough spades to bid game in spades.

Lead: ♡ Q, top of sequence, is best.

Play: Declarer can set up a diamond trick (lead ◇ 7 and force out ◇ A) and ruff the heart losers in dummy before drawing trumps. A club has to be lost, making 11 tricks. Declarer should not draw trumps before ruffing a heart loser in dummy.

Hand 10: Dealer East: North-South vulnerable

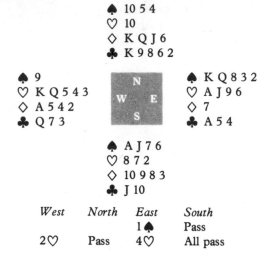

```
                    ♠ 10 5 4
                    ♡ 10
                    ◇ K Q J 6
                    ♣ K 9 8 6 2
  ♠ 9                              ♠ K Q 8 3 2
  ♡ K Q 5 4 3        N             ♡ A J 9 6
  ◇ A 5 4 2       W     E          ◇ 7
  ♣ Q 7 3            S             ♣ A 5 4
                    ♠ A J 7 6
                    ♡ 8 7 2
                    ◇ 10 9 8 3
                    ♣ J 10
```

West	North	East	South
		1♠	Pass
2♡	Pass	4♡	All pass

Bidding: West showed at least 10 points in bidding 2♡ (with only 6-9, raise partner or bid at the one-level). East is worth 17 points in hearts, counting 3 for the singleton, and so bids 4♡. When you have enough for game, do not dally – bid it.

Lead: ◇ K, top of strong sequence.

Play: West wins ◇ A and should lead a spade to the king to set up the ♠ Q as a winner. Later, before drawing trumps, West should ruff diamonds in dummy and discard a club loser on the ♠ Q. Declarer can ruff diamonds in dummy and spades or clubs in hand, making 10 or 11 tricks. When you need to ruff several losers in dummy, do not draw trumps too early.

Hand 11: Dealer South: Both vulnerable

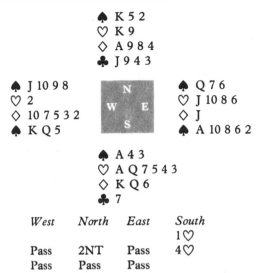

	♠ K 5 2	
	♡ K 9	
	◇ A 9 8 4	
	♣ J 9 4 3	

♠ J 10 9 8		♠ Q 7 6
♡ 2	N	♡ J 10 8 6
◇ 10 7 5 3 2	W E	◇ J
♣ K Q 5	S	♠ A 10 8 6 2

	♠ A 4 3	
	♡ A Q 7 5 4 3	
	◇ K Q 6	
	♣ 7	

West	North	East	South
			1♡
Pass	2NT	Pass	4♡
Pass	Pass	Pass	

Bidding: North's 2NT shows 11-12 points and balanced shape. South thus knows there are enough points for game and at least eight hearts together, since North must have at least two hearts if the hand is balanced. 4♡ is a better prospect, therefore, than 3NT (which could be defeated on a club lead).

Lead: ♠ J, top of sequence.

Play: Win the spade lead and start drawing trumps. After three rounds of trumps, East has a trump winner. When there is one trump out, higher than yours, it is usually best to leave it out and play your other suits. Let them win their trump later.

Hand 12: Dealer West: Nil vulnerable

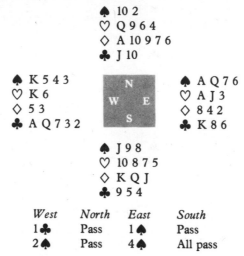

```
                        ♠ 10 2
                        ♡ Q 9 6 4
                        ◇ A 10 9 7 6
                        ♣ J 10

    ♠ K 5 4 3                          ♠ A Q 7 6
    ♡ K 6              N               ♡ A J 3
    ◇ 5 3          W       E           ◇ 8 4 2
    ♣ A Q 7 3 2        S               ♣ K 8 6

                        ♠ J 9 8
                        ♡ 10 8 7 5
                        ◇ K Q J
                        ♣ 9 5 4
```

West	North	East	South
1♣	Pass	1♠	Pass
2♠	Pass	4♠	All pass

Bidding: West opens 1♣, longest suit first. East responds 1♠, promising at least four spades and six or more points. East intends to reach game but is not sure of the best spot. 3NT would be a poor choice of response, since the diamonds are very weak and East has a major suit to show. (Note that 3NT could be defeated on a diamond lead).

Lead: ◇ K, top of sequence.

Play: When East gains the lead, East should draw trumps. Declarer can ruff a diamond loser in dummy or, preferably, discard losers on the club winners by playing dummy's long suit *after* drawing trumps. Making 11 tricks.

Chapter 5

SLAM BIDDING AND TWO-OPENINGS

The main aim of the bidding is to reach a game as long as the partnership has enough points. However, the scoring table gives very substantial rewards for bidding for 12 or 13 tricks and then making contract. A contract of six (12 tricks) is called a small slam and if you bid and make a small slam, you score extra points:

500 points if not vulnerable
750 points if vulnerable

A contract of seven (13 tricks) is called a grand slam and if you bid and make a grand slam, you score extra points:

1000 points if not vulnerable
1500 points if vulnerable

If you could make a slam but fail to bid it, you score no extra points and you have missed the opportunity to obtain a large bonus. On the other hand, if you bid a slam and fail to make the tricks required by your contract, you have also lost a valuable score, since you could have made a game.

26 points makes game a good bet, but for a slam you need more points since more tricks are needed. The guidelines are:

With 33 points or more, bid a small slam. If you choose a suit, you will want to have at least eight good trumps together, or preferably nine.

With 37 points or more, bid a grand slam. If you choose a suit, be confident that you have no losers in the trump suit and at least nine trumps between you and partner. If unsure, prefer to settle for a sure small slam than a risky grand slam.

Examples

♠ A Q 6
♡ K Q 9
♢ A K 5 2
♣ Q J 7

Partner opened 1NT. Your response? Your 21 points plus partner's 12 at least makes a total of 33 or more. Bid 6NT. The maximum combined total is 35 points, not enough to try for a grand slam of 7NT.

♠ A J 8 7 6 4 3
♡ K J 6
♢ - - -
♣ A Q J

Partner opened 1NT. Your response? As opener is balanced, you have at least nine spades together so add your shortage points, five for the void. That gives you 21 points and at least 33 together. Bid 6♠.

♠ - - -
♡ A Q
♢ A K 8 6 4 3
♣ A 9 6 4 3

Suppose you have opened 1♢ to which partner has responded 3♢. What next?

As partner is showing 10-12 points and support for your suit, you can count on at least ten diamonds together and, by counting 5 points for your void and 1 point for your doubleton, your total point count is 23 and with partner's promised values, you have 33 points or more. Your best shot, therefore, is to bid 6♢.

Starting with a two opening

Hands with more than 21 high cards points are too strong to open with just a one-opening, since partner may pass such an opening with 0-5 points. Suppose that you hold this hand:

♠ A K 6
♡ A K 8 7 2
♢ A K Q J
♣ 5

If you were to open this with 1 Heart, imagine your disappointment if the bidding went – Pass, Pass, Pass. If partner held two or three points or even less, partner would be quite right to pass and yet you would have a great chance for game, but after three passes, the bidding is over and you would not be permitted to make another bid to increase the contract.

Most hands with 20 points or more are also too strong to open with a one-bid. Often one winner in partner's hand can produce a game, yet partner with only an ace or a king would pass an opening bid of one. To cope with such powerhouses, we open with a Two-Bid. The actual bid we choose will depend on both the strength of the hand and the shape of the hand.

The 2NT opening shows 20-22 points and balanced shape. Partner may pass this opening with up to three points, but with any chance for game, partner will respond. With a balanced hand, go for no-trumps, while with a long suit or an unbalanced hand, you can bid three-in-a-suit (shows five cards in the suit bid) or bid for game in a major with a six-card or longer suit.

Balanced hands with 23 points or more are opened 2♣.

With a powerful hand which is not balanced, you may open 2 ♣ (an artificial strong opening bid which shows either 23 hcp or more or a hand which contains ten winners or more) *or* you may open 2♠, 2♡ or 2◇ (which are genuine bids showing a hand around the 20-22 point mark in high cards with a long suit, at least five cards).

The 2♣ opening: With a weak hand, 7 points or less, responder bids 2◇, an artificial negative reply, saying nothing about diamonds, but merely confirming a weak hand. If opener bids 2NT over 2◇, this is not forcing and shows a balanced hand of 23-24 points (but responder would bid on to game with 2 points or better). Any other rebid by opener over 2◇ is *forcing to game*. This means both partners must keep bidding until a contract of 3NT, 4♡, 4♠, 5♣ or 5◇ is reached. With your rebid, the normal rules for showing suits apply: longest suit first, higher suit first with two five-card suits up-the-line when holding only four-card suits.

Any response to 2♣ other than 2◇ shows 8 points or more or 1½ tricks or better. Bidding continues until the best contract is found and a slam is highly likely after a positive response.

The 2♠, 2♡ and 2◇ openings: Responder must reply to these openings and the negative reply (0-7 points) in each case is 2NT. Any other response shows 8 points or more and is forcing to at least game. After a negative 2NT response, if opener repeats the first suit or rebids in a lower-ranking suit, responder may now pass, but other rebids by opener demand the responder to make some reply.

Example hands on two openings

Hand 13: Dealer North: Nil vulnerable

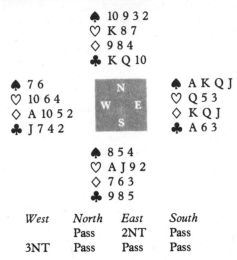

```
                    ♠ 10 9 3 2
                    ♡ K 8 7
                    ◇ 9 8 4
                    ♣ K Q 10

  ♠ 7 6              N            ♠ A K Q J
  ♡ 10 6 4                        ♡ Q 5 3
  ◇ A 10 5 2      W     E         ◇ K Q J
  ♣ J 7 4 2          S            ♣ A 6 3

                    ♠ 8 5 4
                    ♡ A J 9 2
                    ◇ 7 6 3
                    ♣ 9 8 5
```

West	North	East	South
	Pass	2NT	Pass
3NT	Pass	Pass	Pass

Bidding: West might pass an opening one-bid, but has enough opposite the 20-22 shown by 2NT to raise to 3NT.

Lead: ♡2, fourth-highest.

Play: North plays the ♡K, winning, and returns a heart, giving the defenders the first four tricks. Declarer should win the rest. Be careful not to discard a diamond on the fourth round of hearts – a club discard is safe. Win their switch and overtake the third round of diamonds with dummy's ace, giving declarer 4 diamonds, 4 spades and the ace of clubs.

[58]

Hand 14: Dealer East: East-West vulnerable

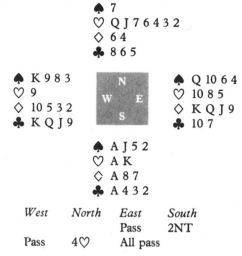

	♠ 7	
	♡ Q J 7 6 4 3 2	
	◇ 6 4	
	♣ 8 6 5	
♠ K 9 8 3		♠ Q 10 6 4
♡ 9		♡ 10 8 5
◇ 10 5 3 2		◇ K Q J 9
♣ K Q J 9		♣ 10 7
	♠ A J 5 2	
	♡ A K	
	◇ A 8 7	
	♣ A 4 3 2	

West	*North*	*East*	*South*
		Pass	2NT
Pass	4♡	All pass	

Bidding: North has enough for game opposite 20-22 points but bids 4♡, not 3NT, since North knows the partnership has at least nine hearts, because the 2NT opening, being balanced, must contain at least two hearts. 3NT would be defeated easily.

Lead: ◇ K, top of strong sequence.

Play: Win the ◇ A, play the ♡ A and ♡ K, cash the ♠ A and ruff a spade in order to get to your hand. Play the ♡ Q to draw the last trump and then take your other winners. Declarer can make ten tricks via seven heart winners and three outside aces. In no-trumps, South would make just five tricks, because South could never reach the winners in the North hand!

Hand 15: Dealer South: Both vulnerable

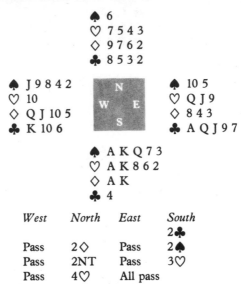

```
                    ♠ 6
                    ♡ 7 5 4 3
                    ◇ 9 7 6 2
                    ♣ 8 5 3 2

    ♠ J 9 8 4 2          N          ♠ 10 5
    ♡ 10            W         E      ♡ Q J 9
    ◇ Q J 10 5          S          ◇ 8 4 3
    ♣ K 10 6                        ♣ A Q J 9 7

                    ♠ A K Q 7 3
                    ♡ A K 8 6 2
                    ◇ A K
                    ♣ 4
```

West	North	East	South
			2♣
Pass	2◇	Pass	2♠
Pass	2NT	Pass	3♡
Pass	4♡	All pass	

Bidding: With 23 hcp, South opens 2♣. North must reply, even with no points, and bids 2◇, the negative reply. South rebids 2♠, the higher suit with a 5-5. The bidding must now continue to game and with no support and no long suit, North rebids 2NT. 3♡ shows the second suit and North raises to 4♡.

Lead: ◇ Q, top of sequence.

Play: Win ◇ A; cash ♡ A and ♡ K to draw trumps; when they do not divide 2-2, leave the last trump out; switch to spades and ruff two spade losers in dummy. Making 11 tricks.

Hand 16: Dealer West: Nil vulnerable

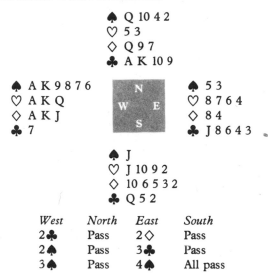

```
                    ♠ Q 10 4 2
                    ♡ 5 3
                    ◇ Q 9 7
                    ♣ A K 10 9
  ♠ A K 9 8 7 6                    ♠ 5 3
  ♡ A K Q          N               ♡ 8 7 6 4
  ◇ A K J      W       E           ◇ 8 4
  ♣ 7              S               ♣ J 8 6 4 3
                    ♠ J
                    ♡ J 10 9 2
                    ◇ 10 6 5 3 2
                    ♣ Q 5 2
```

West	North	East	South
2♣	Pass	2◇	Pass
2♠	Pass	3♣	Pass
3♠	Pass	4♠	All pass

Bidding: With such a powerhouse, West opens 2♣. East must respond and chooses 2◇, the negative response. West shows the spades and without support, East shows the club suit. West rebids the spades to show six (the 2♠ bid already indicated a five-card suit) and this enables East to raise to 4♠.

Lead: ♣K. The standard lead in a trump contract from a suit headed by the A-K is the king. The ace lead denies the king.

Play: West ruffs the second club, cashes the ◇A and ◇K, followed by the ◇J, ruffed in dummy. The ace and king of spades are cashed but spades break badly. Making 10 tricks.

Example hands on slam bidding

Hand 17: Dealer North: Nil vulnerable

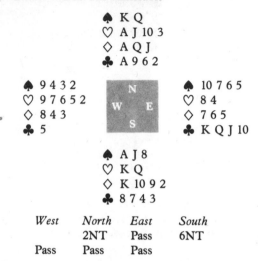

```
                    ♠ K Q
                    ♡ A J 10 3
                    ◇ A Q J
                    ♣ A 9 6 2
   ♠ 9 4 3 2                        ♠ 10 7 6 5
   ♡ 9 7 6 5 2         N            ♡ 8 4
   ◇ 8 4 3         W       E        ◇ 7 6 5
   ♣ 5                 S            ♣ K Q J 10
                    ♠ A J 8
                    ♡ K Q
                    ◇ K 10 9 2
                    ♣ 8 7 4 3
```

West	North	East	South
	2NT	Pass	6NT
Pass	Pass	Pass	

Bidding: As South knows the partnership has 33 points at least, South bids the slam and with a balanced hand, chooses 6NT.

Lead: ♣K, top of strong sequence.

Play: There are several ways to make 12 tricks (via 3 spades, 4 hearts, 4 diamonds and 1 club), but declarer must take care not to have winners marooned in dummy or in hand. One way to succeed, after winning the ♣A, is: ♠K, ♠Q overtaken by ♠A, ♠J cashed; ♡K, ♡Q overtaken by ♡A, ♡J and ♡10; ◇A, ◇Q, ◇J overtaken by ◇K and ◇10 cashed.

Hand 18: Dealer East: North-South vulnerable

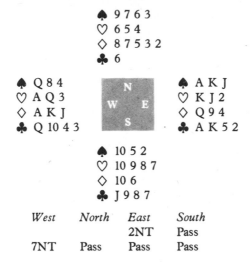

```
                    ♠ 9 7 6 3
                    ♡ 6 5 4
                    ♢ 8 7 5 3 2
                    ♣ 6
  ♠ Q 8 4                              ♠ A K J
  ♡ A Q 3              N               ♡ K J 2
  ♢ A K J         W         E          ♢ Q 9 4
  ♣ Q 10 4 3           S               ♣ A K 5 2
                    ♠ 10 5 2
                    ♡ 10 9 8 7
                    ♢ 10 6
                    ♣ J 9 8 7
```

West	North	East	South
		2NT	Pass
7NT	Pass	Pass	Pass

Bidding: East shows 20-22 points with 2NT and with 18 points, West counts on 38 points or more, making 7NT a good bet.

Lead: ♡ 10, top of sequence.

Play: Even with 39 points, 7NT is no certainty. With 3 spades, 3 hearts and 3 diamonds, declarer needs 4 club tricks. If clubs divide 3-2, there is no problem. To cater for a 4-1 break, declarer must take care to play the ♣A and ♣K first. When North discards on the second club, declarer can capture South's clubs without loss. On the third club, if South plays the 9, declarer can win by playing the 10 (capturing the J with the Q) while if South plays the J, the Q wins now and the 10 wins next.

Hand 19: Dealer South: Both vulnerable

```
                    ♠ K 10 9 4
                    ♡ Q J 10 7 6
                    ◇ 10 8 3
                    ♣ 4
♠ A Q J 8 7 6                        ♠ 3 2
♡ - - -            N                 ♡ K 3
◇ A K           W     E              ◇ J 7 6 5 4
♣ A K Q 9 8        S                 ♣ J 7 5 2
                    ♠ 5
                    ♡ A 9 8 5 4 2
                    ◇ Q 9 2
                    ♣ 10 6 3
```

West	North	East	South
			Pass
2♣	Pass	2◇	Pass
2♠	Pass	3◇	Pass
4♣	Pass	5♣	Pass
6♣	Pass	Pass	Pass

Bidding: West opens 2♣ and shows the longer suit over East's weakness 2◇. Over East's diamonds West rebids to show the second suit. When East raises clubs, West judges that at worst, there might be one loser, in spades, and so bids 6♣.

Lead: ♡ Q, top of sequence.

Play: Ruff the lead and draw trumps. ♠ A then ♠ Q eliminates the king. After regaining the lead, West cashes the ♠ J and ruffs a spade in dummy. West's remaining two spades are winners.

Hand 20: Dealer West: Nil vulnerable

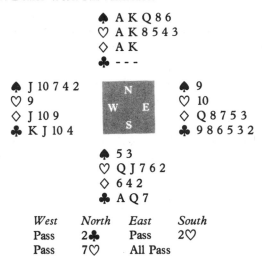

	♠ A K Q 8 6
	♡ A K 8 5 4 3
	◇ A K
	♣ - - -

♠ J 10 7 4 2   ♠ 9
♡ 9   ♡ 10
◇ J 10 9   ◇ Q 8 7 5 3
♣ K J 10 4   ♣ 9 8 6 5 3 2

♠ 5 3
♡ Q J 7 6 2
◇ 6 4 2
♣ A Q 7

West	*North*	*East*	*South*
Pass	2♣	Pass	2♡
Pass	7♡	All Pass	

Bidding: North opens 2♣ to show a powerhouse. South has a positive response and bids 2♡, a most pleasant surprise for North. It is clear to North that there is an excellent trump fit, as South will hold four hearts and may have more. As there should be no losers in any suit, North bids 7♡ without further ado. (Note that the 7NT grand slam should fail.)

Lead: ◇ J, sequence is safest against a grand slam.

Play: Win ◇ A and draw trumps in one round. Then play the top spades, keeping a count of them. After three rounds, there are still two spades out. Ruff the spade losers in your hand and you have 13 tricks. The ♣A is not even needed!

Chapter 6

OTHER ASPECTS OF BIDDING

The preceding chapters will teach you how to play bridge in just a few hours. If you study the chapters carefully, you can get along reasonably well with what you know. There is more to bidding and play, however, than you will find in this elementary introduction and how to improve your game and where to practice and what books to study is outlined in the section 'Where To Next?' which begins on page 79. A brief outline is given here of some other bidding techniques which you are likely to come across when you play and which you will need to learn in the subsequent development of your skills.

Opening bids of three and four

Opening bids at the three-level or higher are played as *weak* openings based on a long, strong suit. The normal point range for these openings is 6-10 HCP and a seven-card suit for the three-level or an eight-card suit for the four-level. Even opening bids of 5♣ or 5♦ are played as weak, based on 6-10 HCP and an eight-card or nine-card suit. The 3NT opening shows a 7-card or longer minor suit headed by the A-K-Q.

These are called 'pre-emptive' openings because the purpose is to shut out the opposition. A pre-empt should be within three tricks of the bid not vulnerable and two tricks if vulnerable.

Overcalls and jump-overcalls

There is only one opening bid in each auction, the first bid. The side that does not open the bidding is called the 'defending' side and a suit bid or a no-trump bid by the defenders is known as an 'overcall'.

The 1NT overcall shows 16-18 points, balanced shape and a stopper in the enemy suit. A stopper is a high card which can prevent the opponents from cashing a suit from the top. The ace is obviously a stopper and K-x, Q-x-x and J-x-x-x are considered the minimum requirements for a stopper. (An 'x' is any card below a ten, any worthless card, a 'rag'.) The 1NT overcall is stronger than a 1NT opening, while overcalls in a suit may be significantly weaker than an opening bid in a suit.

A suit overcall does not require 12 points. You may overcall with considerably less than that. What is needed is a strong five-card or longer suit, normally with two or three top honours. At the one-level, a suit overcall shows 8-15 HCP and the strong five-card suit. At the two-level, the range is 10-15 HCP and the strong five-card suit. The powerful suit is essential.

A jump-overcall in a suit shows a five-card or longer suit with two or three top honours and about 16-19 HCP. It is not a forcing bid but it encourages partner to try for a game.

A pre-emptive overcall is a jump-overcall which skips two or more levels, e.g. (1♡): 3♠ or (1♡): 4♣. It is a weak bid, based on about 6-10 HCP and a seven-card or eight-card suit.

Penalty doubles *v.* takeout doubles

You may at your turn to bid double a bid of the opponents. You simply say 'Double'. The primary aim of a double is to increase the penalties when the opponents fail in their contract. A bid following a double cancels the double (as it cancels any other bid) but does not prevent a subsequent double. You may redouble an opponent's double and if this becomes the final bid, then if declarer succeeds, declarer scores four times as many points as usual while if declarer fails, the penalties are far more severe than usual (see the Scoring Table).

When a double is meant for penalties, partner is requested to pass. A double is for penalties in standard methods when it occurs at the three-level or higher *or* when it is a double of a bid of no-trumps *or* if it occurs after partner has made a bid.

We also use what is called a 'takeout double'. This is a request for partner to bid, to take out the double, to remove it by making a bid. A double is for takeout if it is a double of a suit bid at the one-level or two-level. It is vital to understand the difference between the two kinds of doubles since the penalty double asks you to pass and the takeout double asks you to bid.

A takeout double should have about the equivalent strength of an opening bid, should be short in the opponents' suit and should have three-card or four-card support for the unbid suits. The takeout double is forcing and with a very weak hand, partner bids a suit (0–9 points) or 1NT (6-9 points).

The Blackwood Convention

'Blackwood' is a bid of 4NT which asks partner, "How many aces do you have?" There are four possible answers:

$$5\clubsuit = 0 \text{ or } 4 \text{ aces}$$
$$5\diamondsuit = 1 \text{ ace}$$
$$5\heartsuit = 2 \text{ aces}$$
$$5\spadesuit = 3 \text{ aces}$$

After the answer to 4NT, a bid of 5NT asks for kings, and the answers follow in a similar pattern ($6\clubsuit$ = no king, $6\diamondsuit$ = 1, $6\heartsuit$ = 2, $6\spadesuit$ = 3 and 6NT = 4 kings). 4NT to ask for aces is used when you know you have enough points for a slam and you also know which suit is going to be trumps. The 4NT bidder is the one who makes the decision as to the final contract. The 5NT ask for kings is used if you have enough to try for a grand slam and the partnership is known to hold all the aces.

The Stayman convention

After an opening bid of 1NT, a response of 2♣ is used as a question: "Do you have a four-card major suit?" The answers:

$$2\diamondsuit = \text{No major suit}$$
$$2\heartsuit = \text{I have four hearts}$$
$$2\spadesuit = \text{I have four spades}$$

If the 1NT opener has both majors, show the hearts first.

Use the Stayman 2♣ convention when you hold at least one four-card major and eleven or more points. 2NT: 3♣ is used the same way with at least one major and four or more points.

Chapter 7

TIPS ON DECLARER PLAY

FOR NO-TRUMPS:
1. Count your instant winners.
2. Decide which suit will provide the extra tricks needed.
3. Play that suit and do not worry about giving up the lead.
4. Set up the extra tricks first, cash your sure winners later.

FOR TRUMPS CONTRACTS:
1. Count your losers, suit by suit, based on your own hand.
2. See which losers are covered by winning cards in dummy.
3. If you have too many losers, check whether you can ruff losers in dummy or discard them on extra winners in dummy.
4. It is normally correct to draw trumps early. However, do not draw trumps straight away if you need a quick discard or if you need dummy's trumps to ruff your losers.
5. Prefer to trump losers in the shorter trump hand. You rarely gain a trick by trumping in the long trump hand.
6. If there is one trump out, draw it if it is lower than yours but if it is higher, normally leave it out and tackle the other suits.

The hold-up play
In no-trumps, if you hold A-x-x and dummy has x-x or x-x-x, you should normally hold off with your ace until the third round, unless there is some other suit which is even more dangerous. The hold-up play is rarely necessary in a trump contract.

High-card-from-shortage
Where you have winners in both hands, play the winners first from the hand with fewer cards (the short hand). For example, if dummy has two cards and you have three, play dummy's winners first. This enables you to take all the tricks to which you are entitled and will prevent suits being blocked.

[69]

DECLARER	DUMMY	
A-K-Q-2	J-5	Play the jack and the two first.

The same principle applies when you are knocking out an ace:

DECLARER	DUMMY	
K-Q-4	J-10-5-2	Play the king first, queen next.

Count the missing cards

All good players keep track of the cards that are missing in each suit. This is a tough task when you are just learning but with practice you will become quite proficient at it. Start by counting just the missing cards in the trump suit or in your longest suit in no-trumps. Once you have mastered that, you can extend your skill to the next longest suit and before long, you will be able to do it in all four suits.

The best way to count the cards is to work out as soon as dummy appears how many cards the opponents hold in the critical suit. If you and dummy have 8, they have 5; if you and dummy have 9, they have 4, and so on. Then you simply concentrate on the cards they play and deduct that each time. With regular practice, this will become second nature to you.

Chapter 8

TIPS ON DEFENDING

Opening leads against no-trumps

Lead your long suit against no-trumps, unless partner has bid a suit (prefer to lead partner's suit) or the opponents have bid your long suit (prefer to lead some other suit). The card to lead in your long suit is the top card from a three-card or longer sequence (lead the Q from Q-J-10-5-2), but when you do not have a sequence, lead fourth-highest (the 5 from K-J-7-5-2).

Opening leads against trumps

The long suit is no longer so appealing, since the opponents may be able to trump in on the second or third round of the suit. A short suit lead is usually more appealing since you will be able to ruff as soon as you become void in the suit. If partner has bid a suit, prefer to lead that suit. If partner has not bid, avoid leading a suit bid by the opposition. The best leads are suits headed by a three-card sequence, a suit headed by A-K or a singleton lead. Leads to avoid are from suits headed by the ace without the king, doubleton honours such as K-x. Q-x or J-x when partner has not bid the suit or singleton trump leads.

The card to lead from a long suit is the same as in no-trumps, top from a three-card or longer sequence or fourth-highest when you do not hold such a sequence, but there are three exceptions to this approach:

1. From A-K-x-x-x-, lead fourth-highest against no-trumps, but lead the king against a suit contract.

2. From K-Q-x-x-x, lead fourth-highest against no-trumps, but lead the king against a suit contract.

3. From A-x-x-x-x, lead fourth-highest against no-trumps. Against suit contracts, try to avoid leading a suit headed by the ace, but if you must lead the suit, lead the ace, not a low one.

When leading a short suit:

1. Lead top card from a doubleton (the 8 from 8-6).

2. From a tripleton, lead the top card from a three-card or two-card sequence headed by an honour (the Q from Q-J-5), lead the bottom card when you hold an honour card or two honours not in sequence (the 5 from Q-9-5) and lead the middle card when you hold no honour card (the 7 from 8-7-3).

Defence after the opening lead

It is often best to play second hand low and third hand high, but these rules need to be tempered to the situation. It is normal to return your partner's lead, but be prepared to switch to another suit if your suit is very strong or if returning partner's suit is clearly futile. It is generally not a good idea to lead a suit which dummy can trump. 'Cover an honour with an honour' is good advice only if this would build up a trick for your side. High-card-then-low-card is a signal asking partner to continue playing that suit. Lowest card (or lowest discard) asks partner to discontinue that suit and switch to some other suit.

Example hands on defending

Hand 21: Dealer North: Nil vulnerable

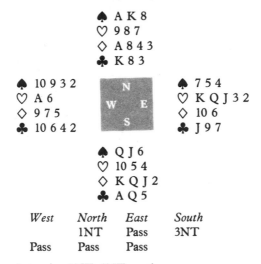

	♠ A K 8	
	♡ 9 8 7	
	◇ A 8 4 3	
	♣ K 8 3	

♠ 10 9 3 2		♠ 7 5 4
♡ A 6		♡ K Q J 3 2
◇ 9 7 5		◇ 10 6
♣ 10 6 4 2		♣ J 9 7

	♠ Q J 6	
	♡ 10 5 4	
	◇ K Q J 2	
	♣ A Q 5	

West	North	East	South
	1NT	Pass	3NT
Pass	Pass	Pass	

Bidding: A routine 1NT: 3NT auction.

Lead: ♡ K, top of sequence.

Play: The contract will be defeated if West overtakes the ♡ K lead with the ace and returns the 6 of hearts. East wins and continues hearts, enabling the defence to take the first five tricks. If West plays low at trick one, declarer can make 10 tricks. West should realise from the *king* that East has the K-Q-J and thus appreciate that by playing low in hearts, only two tricks will be taken; by overtaking you will take more.

Hand 22: Dealer East: Nil vulnerable

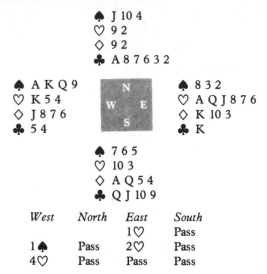

                        ♠ J 10 4
                        ♡ 9 2
                        ◇ 9 2
                        ♣ A 8 7 6 3 2

♠ A K Q 9   ♠ 8 3 2
♡ K 5 4   N   ♡ A Q J 8 7 6
◇ J 8 7 6   W   E   ◇ K 10 3
♣ 5 4   S   ♣ K

                        ♠ 7 6 5
                        ♡ 10 3
                        ◇ A Q 5 4
                        ♣ Q J 10 9

West	North	East	South
		1♡	Pass
1♠	Pass	2♡	Pass
4♡	Pass	Pass	Pass

Bidding: West bids 1♠, up-the-line with four-card suits and supports the hearts when East shows a long suit.

Lead: ♣Q, top of sequence.

Play: North should win the ♣A since the ♣Q denies the king. When East's ♣K falls, North should realise that declarer has no more clubs and would ruff a club continuation. It is also clear by looking at dummy that a spade switch would be futile. Therefore, shift to the *nine* of diamonds (top from a doubleton) and after South wins two diamonds, a third diamond can be ruffed by North to defeat the contract.

Hand 23: Dealer South: Nil vulnerable

```
              ♠ Q J 5
              ♡ 8 5 4
              ◇ A K Q 9 5
              ♣ 8 3
♠ 4 3 2            N            ♠ 10
♡ Q 9 2       W       E        ♡ A K 10 6 3
◇ 10 8 7 6         S           ◇ 4 2
♣ A Q 9                        ♣ 7 6 5 4 2
              ♠ A K 9 8 7 6
              ♡ J 7
              ◇ J 3
              ♣ K J 10
```

West	North	East	South
			1♠
Pass	2◇	Pass	2♠
Pass	4♠	All pass	

Lead: ♡2, bottom from 3 to an honour. West should not lead a diamond (dummy bid the suit) or a club (avoid leading a suit headed by the ace in a trump contract). On a diamond lead, South makes 11 tricks and at least 10 on the ♣A lead.

Play: East wins two hearts and realises from West's play of 2-9 in hearts that West has the last heart. With 9-2 doubleton, West would have played the 9 first, 2 next. Leading high-low indicates a doubleton. As declarer would ruff the next heart, East switches to ♣4 and the defenders take the first four tricks. If East plays a third heart, South can make 11 tricks.

Hand 24: Dealer West: Nil vulnerable

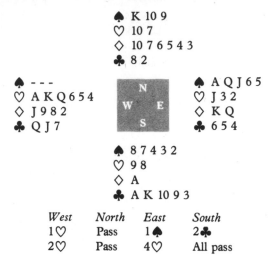

	♠ K 10 9	
	♡ 10 7	
	◇ 10 7 6 5 4 3	
	♣ 8 2	

♠ - - -		♠ A Q J 6 5
♡ A K Q 6 5 4		♡ J 3 2
◇ J 9 8 2		◇ K Q
♣ Q J 7		♣ 6 5 4

	♠ 8 7 4 3 2	
	♡ 9 8	
	◇ A	
	♣ A K 10 9 3	

West	North	East	South
1♡	Pass	1♠	2♣
2♡	Pass	4♡	All pass

Bidding: South's suit is strong enough to overcall. West could rebid 2◇ but the hearts are so much stronger and longer.

Lead: ♣8, top from a doubleton. Even without South's bid, the doubleton club is appealing. The weaker the hand, the more attractive it is to lead a short suit since partner then figures to have entries to give you ruffs. A spade lead gives West 11 tricks.

Play: South can win ♣K-A and, as North shows a doubleton, play a third club for North to ruff. This puts the contract one down, but South can do even better: win the top clubs, cash the ◇ A (create your own void), then give North a club ruff and receive a diamond ruff to beat 4♡ by two tricks.

Chapter 9

THE WORLD OF BRIDGE

There are two different forms of contract bridge. Rubber bridge (or social bridge) is played mainly in private homes and in a few clubs. The aim is to win rubbers and the scoring is according to the table on page 91. The most important feature is that what you score on one deal carries forward to the next deal until the rubber is concluded.

Duplicate bridge (or competitive bridge) is played mainly in bridge clubs. Each deal is independent and you are rewarded when you make a partscore or a game by extra bonuses (50 for a partscore, 300 for a game not vulnerable, 500 for a game vulnerable). Honours do not count. A duplicate game has a 'director', who has a number of functions, including organising the game, ruling on any infractions and scoring the results.

At the start of a duplicate session, the cards are shuffled and dealt, but thereafter there is no more shuffling and dealing. You play your cards in front of you (not into the middle of the table) and at the end of a hand, you return your cards to the correct position in the 'board' (card container). This allows other pairs to play exactly the same deals as you have played. You play against different opponents on each round and a round consists normally of two or three deals. After each round, you meet new opponents and the boards are moved to new tables.

There are two main types of duplicate tournaments, pairs events and teams events. An individual tournament is held occasionally (usually no more than once a year in each club or county) where you change partners, opponents and boards after each round. At club level, most events are pairs games where you play with the same partner throughout the event. At county and national level, there is a roughly even division of pairs and teams games and at international level, most events are contested by teams, representing their country.

In a team event, you compete against one other team at a time. A

[77]

team consists of four, five or six players but only four members play at any one time. At one table Team A sits North-South while Team B sits East-West. After a board is completed, it goes to the other table where the other Team A pair sits East-West and the other Team B pair sits North-South. There is thus a direct comparison between the results obtained by each team on each deal. This is the fairest kind of tournament, since your score is not affected by any results other than your own and the luck factor is eliminated.

The World Bridge Federation was formed in 1958 and has about 80 members including the People's Republic of China (since 1980) but not Russia. The WBF organises world championships each year, teams events every year and a pairs event every four years. From 1957 to 1975 Italy dominated the world championships and since then world titles have been won by Brazil, France, Poland and the United States. The USA has more top players than any other country.

WHERE TO NEXT?

You should start playing as soon as possible, preferably with a group of friends of about the same standard. If you can arrange to be supervised and encouraged by a sympathetic and competent player, so much the better.

Do not be discouraged if you are slow in remembering all the rules and the number of points needed for various bids. With a little practice, they will become second nature to you. After playing some games, it will be worthwhile to read this book carefully again. Some of the points that you may have forgotten will be refreshed and some other points may now make more sense to you. After a few more games, another reading will not go amiss. A handy quick-reference flipper guide which you will find useful is the *Basic Acol Bridge Flipper*.

After playing for two to six months, you will be ready for a more comprehensive textbook. Recommended is *Basic Bridge* which covers all the standard material you will need at this early stage. It also has an accompanying reference guide, the *Acol Bridge Flipper*. There are many good bridge books – concentrate initially on those dealing with card play.

As most cities have several bridge clubs and most towns of any size have a bridge club, you should be able to find a bridge club reasonably handy. Once you can play at the standard of this book, you should consider joining a bridge club if you wish to improve your game. A large bridge club is best if available, since it will provide classes conducted by a competent teacher, play sessions supervised by a good teacher or player, and special sessions for novice players only. Supervised play sessions are excellent while you are still learning.

It is best not to play against very strong players until you have had a fair amount of experience. Their methods may confuse you and strong players tend to play much too quickly for novices, making it harder to follow what is going on and not giving you enough time to work out your best play. If you feel timid about playing in experienced company, you can still learn a good deal by watching strong players in action. Do not say anything during the game, but concentrate on just one player's cards and try to decide what you would bid or play before the player makes that decision and see whether your actions match the player's. After a hand is over, most good players do not mind if you ask them a question or two.

If asked to have a game, do not refuse but explain that you are still a novice. If you are lucky, you may have a partner who is better than you and can point out your mistakes kindly. Try to find another enthusiastic player of about your own standard so that you can compete together in the club events, discuss what happens at the tournaments and improve together.

If you are a schoolboy or schoolgirl, find out whether your school has a bridge club. If not, you might find other students with whom you could start a school club. There are some inter-school competitions but do not become overzealous with your bridge. Your schoolwork is still more important, but you can combine it with a healthy interest in bridge.

Appendix 1

THE MECHANICS AND RULES OF BRIDGE – HOW THE GAME IS PLAYED

This section will help to dispel any doubts you might have about the rules or details when playing bridge.

Bridge is a game for four players, playing in two partnerships. It represents a head-to-head battle – your side against their side. Partners sit opposite each other. Partnerships are chosen by agreement or by lot. The most common method is for each player to choose a card from the pack fanned out face down, with the players selecting the two highest cards as one partnership against the players selecting the two lowest cards. After a rubber has been completed, new partnerships are selected.

The bridge pack
A regular pack of 52 cards is used and there are no jokers and no cards of any exceptional rank or function.

There are four suits:

♠ SPADES   ♡ HEARTS   ♢ DIAMONDS   ♣ CLUBS

Each suit consists of thirteen cards which in order of rank are: A, K, Q, J, 10, 9, 8, 7, 6, 5, 4, 3, 2. An ace beats a king, a king beats a queen, a queen beats a jack, a jack beats a ten and so on. The top five cards in each suit, namely the A, K, Q, J and 10, are known as the honour cards or honours.

The suits also have a ranking order: CLUBS (♣) is the *lowest* suit, then come DIAMONDS (♢) and HEARTS (♡) to the highest ranking suit, SPADES (♠). NO-TRUMPS ranks higher than any suit. The order of the suits – C, D, H, S, – is no accident. They are in alphabetical order.

When selecting partnerships, if two cards of the same rank are chosen (e.g. two eights) and the tie needs to be broken, it is decided by suit order (e.g. the ♢ 8 would outrank the ♣ 8).

Dealing

The person who drew the highest card is the dealer on the first hand and has the right to choose seats and the pack of cards with which to deal. The next dealer will be the person on the left of the previous dealer and so on, in clockwise rotation.

The cards are shuffled by the person on the dealer's left. The dealer passes the pack across the table to the person on the dealer's right to be cut. The dealer than deals the cards, one at a time, face down, in clockwise direction, starting with the player on the left, until all 52 cards are dealt, 13 each.

It is courteous to leave your cards face down until the dealer has finished dealing. A misdeal may be corrected if the players have not seen the cards. While the dealer is dealing, the partner of the dealer is shuffling the other pack in preparation for the next deal. Two packs are used in order to speed up the game. After the shuffling is finished the cards are put down on the shuffler's right, ready for the next dealer to pick up.

The start of play

When you pick up your 13 cards, you sort them into suits. It is normal to separate the red suits and black suits so that you can easily see where one suit ends and the next suit begins.

The bidding starts with the dealer. After the bidding is over, the side that has bid higher wins the right to play the hand. One member of this side, called the declarer, plays the hand while the opponents defend the hand. The person on the left of the declarer makes the opening lead. The partner of the declarer, called the dummy, now puts all thirteen cards face up on the table and arranged in suits. The dummy takes no further part in the play, declarer playing both hands. Each player can see 26 cards, the 13 in hand plus the 13 in dummy.

Declarer plays one of the cards from dummy, then the third player plays a card and so does declarer. The four cards now face up on the table are called a *trick*. A trick always consists of four cards played in clockwise sequence, one from each hand.

Each deal in bridge is a battle over thirteen tricks, declarer trying to win as many as nominated in the bidding, while the defenders try to win enough tricks to defeat declarer. A trick is won by the highest card played. The player who wins the trick gathers the four cards together, puts them face down neatly and then leads to the next trick, and so on until all thirteen tricks have been played. (In tournament bridge, called 'duplicate', the cards are not gathered together. Each player keeps their own cards in front of them.)

Following suit

The player who plays the highest ranking card *of the suit led* wins the trick. What if two or more cards of the same rank are played to one trick, who wins then? The basic rule of play is: YOU MUST FOLLOW SUIT, i.e. you must play a card of the same suit as the suit led. If hearts are led, then you must play a heart if you have one and the trick is won by the highest heart played. So that if the two of hearts is led, and the other cards on the trick are the ten of hearts, the queen of spades and the ace of clubs, the trick is won by the ten of hearts. If you are unable to follow suit, you may play any other card at all, but remember it is the highest card of the first suit which wins. If the king of spades is led, it will do you no good to play the ace of clubs – only the ace of spades beats the king of spades.

Trumps

There is one exception to this. Where one of the four suits is, in the bidding, made the *trump* suit, then any card in the trump suit is higher than any card, even an ace, in one of the other suits. So if hearts are trumps, the two of hearts would beat the ace of clubs even when clubs are led. But, first and foremost, you must follow suit. Only when you are out of a suit can you beat a high card of another suit with a trump.

If you are unable to follow suit, you are allowed to trump, *but it is not obligatory*. You may choose to discard and if, for example, partner has already won the trick, it may be foolish to trump partner's winner.

A trick that does not contain a trump is won by the highest card in the suit led. A trick that contains a trump is won by the highest trump in the trick. If you fail to follow suit when able to do so, you have 'revoked' (or 'reneged'). The penalty for a revoke is to transfer one or two tricks to the other side, one trick if you do not win the revoking trick, two tricks if you do win the revoking trick.

The Bidding

The play is preceded by the bidding, also called 'the auction'. Just as in an auction an item goes to the highest bidder, so in the bridge auction each side tries to outbid the other for the right to be declarer and play the hand.

The dealer makes the first bid, then the player on dealer's left and so on in clockwise rotation. Each player may pass (say "No Bid") or make a bid. A player who has previously passed may still make a bid later in the auction. A bid consists of a number (1, 2, 3, 4, 5, 6 or 7) followed by a suit or no-trumps, e.g. three hearts, two spades, four no-trumps, seven diamonds. 'No-Trumps' means that there is to be no trump suit on the deal.

Whenever a bid is made, the bidder is stating the number of tricks *above six* intended to be won in the play. The minimum number of tricks that you may contract for is seven. A bid of 1 Club contracts to make seven tricks with clubs as trumps. The number in the bid is the number of tricks to be won *over and above six tricks*. (Six tricks is not even halfway and you have to bid for more than half the tricks.) The final bid is the 'contract'.

If all players pass without a bid on the first round, there is no play, there is no score, the cards are thrown in and the next dealer deals a new hand. When a player makes a bid on the first round, the auction has started and will be won by the side that bids higher. The auction continues, with each player making a bid or passing, and concludes as soon as a bid is followed by three passes. The side that bids higher sets the trump suit (or no-trumps) and the number of tricks to be won in the play; this is set by the final bid and the member of the side who first bid the trump suit (or no-trumps) becomes the declarer.

After a bid, any player in turn may make a *higher* bid. A bid is higher than a previous bid if it is a larger number than the previous bid, or the same number but in a higher ranking denomination. The order of ranking is:

NO-TRUMPS

SPADES

HEARTS

DIAMONDS

CLUBS

A bid of 1 Heart is higher than a bid of 1 Club. If you want to bid clubs and the previous bid was 2 Spades, you would have to bid 3 Clubs. 2 Clubs would not be higher than 2 Spades.

Game and rubber

A rubber of bridge is over when one side wins two games. A game is won by scoring 100 or more points when declarer.

It is vital to understand how the game is scored, for this affects both the bidding and the play. Your aim is to score more points than the opposition. You may score points: (1) by bidding and making a contract as declarer (s) by defeating the opponents at their contract (3) by earning bonus points.

Some points are written above the line, some below the line on the scoresheet. When adding up the totals, all points count equally, but points below the line are especially valuable, since these are the only points that count towards game. *Only the declarer side can score points for game.* That is the incentive for bidding higher than the opponents. *You score points below the line by bidding and making a contract*, according to this table:

NO-TRUMPS (NT)	40 points for the first trick (over six), 30 for each subsequent trick.
♠ SPADES ♡ HEARTS	30 points for each trick (over six), *in the major suits.*
◊ DIAMONDS ♣ CLUBS	20 points for each trick (over six), *in the minor suits.*

Since game is 100 points or more, it takes a bid of 5 Clubs or 5 Diamonds to make game in the minors, while a bid of 4 Hearts or 4 Spades or more will score game in the majors. In no-trumps, it takes a bid of only 3NT to score a game.

The declaring side gets credit for the tricks it has taken, *but only for the tricks bid and then taken.* So if 4 ♡ is bid, and declarer makes 9 tricks, declarer does not get credit for 9 tricks but suffers a penalty for failing, by one trick, to make the contract.

Thus accuracy in bidding distinguishes contract bridge from auction bridge (where you are given credit for what you make, even if you did not bid it) and becomes the single most important element in the game's winning strategy.

If declarer makes more tricks than the contract calls for, the extra tricks ('overtricks') are not lost, but are scored as bonuses *above the line* – they do not count towards game.

Only points scored by winning the actual number of tricks of the contract are written below the line and only points below the line count towards winning games and the rubber.

A score below the line of less than 100 is called a *part-score*. You may combine two or more part-scores to score the 100 points for game. You cannot carry forward any points over and above 100 to the next game. After one side scores a game, a line is drawn across both columns and both sides start again from zero towards the next game. So, if you have a part-score but the enemy score a game before you have been able to convert your part-score into a game, you have to start again from zero for the next game . . . they have *underlined* you.

Doubles and redoubles

In the bidding, any player may at his turn double a bid made by an opponent. Say 'Double'. If there is no further bidding, the double increases the rewards for success and the penalties for failure. After a double, the other side may redouble (say 'Redouble'), increasing the rewards and penalties further.

Any double or redouble is cancelled by a bid, but there may be further doubles and redoubles of later bids. 1 ♠ making 7 tricks scores 30 below the line, but 1 ♠ doubled and redoubled making 7 tricks scores 120 below the line (and game!), plus 50 bonus points for making a doubled contract ('for the insult').

Other scoring

It is important to get to know the scoring, but since there is a lot of it, you need not learn it all at once. There is a complete scoring table on page 91 to which you can refer if in doubt. *You should know the trick value of each suit and no-trumps* as set out above, and

[86]

you should also know some of the more common scores which go above the line, but the rest of the scoring can be learned gradually, as you play.

As soon as a side has scored a game they are said to be vulnerable and need only one more game to complete the rubber. Penalties are more severe for failing to make a contract when vulnerable than when not vulnerable.

When one side fails to make its contract, the other side scores points above the line as follows:

The declarer side is not vulnerable: 50 points per undertrick.

The declarer side is vulnerable: 100 points per undertrick.

If the final contract is doubled or redoubled, the penalties are more severe (see the scoring table, page 91). Note that penalties are the same no matter what the contract is. One down in 2 ♡ is the same score as one down in 7NT.

You may score bonus points for finishing the rubber. If you end the rubber, you score above the line:

700 points if the opponent are not vulnerable (2 games to 0).

500 points if the opponents are vulnerable (2 games to 1).

You score bonus points for making overtricks in a doubled or redoubled contract (see scoring table) and also for being lucky enough to hold good cards, for holding 'honours'. The honour cards are the A, K, Q, J and 10. You score above the line:

150 points for all 5 trump honours in one hand.

100 points for any 4 of the 5 trump honours in one hand.

150 points for 4 aces in one hand, but only if the contract is NT.

The 100 or 150 bonus for honours is scored whether or not the contract is made. Honours may be held by declarer, dummy or either defender. In order not to tell the opposition what cards you hold, honours are usually claimed after the hand has been played. Honours are not part of the scoring when playing tournament bridge ('duplicate').

A contract of six (12 tricks) is called a small slam and if you *bid and make* a small slam, you score above the line:

500 points if not vulnerable.

750 points if vulnerable.

A contract of seven (13 tricks) is called a grand slam, and if you *bid and make* a grand slam, you score above the line:

1000 points if not vulnerable.

1500 points if vulnerable.

The score for the rubber is entered next to each player's name on a tally card and the next rubber is then started, either with the same partnerships or by drawing again for new partners. Bridge may be played without stakes or with stakes. The amount of the stakes will be by agreement among the players. The stakes are usually stipulated at so much per hundred points, e.g. 10p per hundred or one pound per hundred and agreed before play commences.

The aim of the game

The aim in bridge is to score more points than the opponents. The central feature is *the game*. If the partnership hands can produce a game and game is not bid, a valuable score has been lost. Similarly, if the partnership hands can produce a slam but slam is not bid, again a valuable score has been lost.

If the opposition bid and make a game or a slam, while you could have bid higher than their contract, even though you would have been defeated in your contract, you would have been better off to bid higher if the penalty for defeat would have been less than the value of their contract. Rather accept a small loss (a 'sacrifice') than let the opposition score a game or a slam.

You need not succeed in every game you bid. The rewards for finishing a rubber are so great that failing now and again is no tragedy and a failure rate in games of 1 in 4 is normal and expected. Suppose that you bid 3NT four times and fail on two occasions but succeed on two occasions. Your success rate is only 50% but you are some 700 points in front. The moral is: Do not fret if you do not make every contract you bid.

A comparison of two rubbers

(A)

WE	THEY
700 (2)	
90 (2)	
20 (1)	
100 (1)	
100 (2)	

(B)

WE	THEY
700 (2)	
750 (2)	
500 (1)	
120 (1)	
190 (2)	

A: (1) 5♣, 12 tricks (2) 3NT, 12 tricks Total: 1010, (+10)

B: (1) 6♣, 12 tricks (2) 6NT, 12 tricks Total: 2260, (+23)

Note that the tricks taken were the same for each pair but Pair B won more than twice as much as Pair A because Pair B bid their slams and won 500 and 750 extra bonus points. If you fail to bid an available slam, you have missed a large bonus.

Bridge behaviour and ethics

Bridge has a code of laws which includes a section on the proprieties which deals with proper behaviour at the bridge table. Table talk (anything other than the legal bids) is not welcome in a serious game. In particular, it is the height of rudeness to criticise partner or the opponents. You should be on your best behaviour at the bridge table at all times and a friendly, cheerful disposition will make you a welcome addition to any game. Above all, bridge is meant to be fun.

RUBBER BRIDGE SCORING TABLE

POINTS TOWARDS GAME UNDER THE LINE:

No-trumps – First trick above six 40
                Each additional trick 30
Spades or Hearts (major suits) 30
Diamonds or Clubs (minor suits) 20
Final contract doubled and made: Double above values
Final contract redoubled and made: Above values × 4

BONUS POINTS ABOVE THE LINE:

OVERTRICKS		*Not vul.*	*Vul.*
For each	Not doubled	Trick value	Trick value
overtrick	Doubled	100	200
	Redoubled	200	400

SLAMS BID AND MADE:	*Not vul.*	*Vul.*
Small slam	500	750
Grand slam	1000	1500

FOR DEFEATING A CONTRACT:

Not doubled, each undertrick is 50 not vul., 100 vulnerable
Doubled but not vulnerable, 1st undertrick 100, others 200
Doubled and vulnerable, 1st undertrick 200, others 300
Redoubled: All undertricks score at twice the doubled rate

FOR MAKING A DOUBLED CONTRACT OR A REDOUBLED CONTRACT:
50 ('for the insult')

FOR HONOURS:

Four trumps honours in one hand 100
Five trump honours in one hand 150
Four aces in one hand if contract is NT 150
(Either side can score honours which are claimed at the conclusion
of play).

FOR WINNING THE RUBBER:

For winning by two games to nil 700
For winning by two games to one 500
For one game if rubber is unfinished 300
For partscore if rubber is unfinished 50

Do you ever forget a vital bid or lead?

IF SO, SEE PAGE 95

IMPROVE YOUR BRIDGE MEMORY

by

Ron Klinger

*Everyone can benefit from a study of this book,
for a bridge player with a trained memory
cannot fail to be a better bridge player.*